Lifelong Learning
Theological Education and Supervision

Lifelong Learning

Theological Education and Supervision

Frances Ward

British Library Cataloguing in Publication data

A catalogue record for this book is available
from the British Library

0 334 02962 7

First published in 2005 by SCM Press
9–17 St Albans Place, London N1 0NX

www.scm-canterburypress.co.uk

SCM Press is a division of
SCM-Canterbury Press Ltd

Printed and bound in Great Britain by
William Clowes Ltd, Beccles, Suffolk

CONTENTS

Acknowledgements   vii

Preface   xi

Introduction   1

1 Learning to Read the Signs of the Times:
   Ministry in a Changing World   51

2 What Kind of Learning? Developments within
   Theological Education   65

3 Learning to Play: The Interplay of Theology   87

4 Learning to Listen: The Practice of Supervision   105

5 Learning to Write: The Living Human Document   129

6 Learning to Learn: Resistances Good and Bad   153

7 Learning to Cope with the Downside   173

Conclusion   182

Bibliography   185

Index of Names and Subjects   189

ACKNOWLEDGEMENTS

Who knows when a book starts? This one has been shaping itself over about ten years and has been helped along its way by a great many people. First of all I have to thank John Foskett and David Lyall for encouraging me to revisit and develop the themes of their *Helping the Helpers*, and their guidance in the preparation of this text. Others too have been conversation partners: those members of the Anglican clergy of the diocese of Manchester who have played along with 'the Training Incumbent's Course' over the last five years; Heather Walton, who has invited me to Glasgow to lead sessions with her postgraduate students; and then the following to whom many thanks for (most importantly) their friendship, and also for various ways in which they contributed: John Applegate (especially for his proof-reading expertise); Geoff Babb; James Barnett; Jan Berry; Simone Bennett; Helen Cameron; Jean Coates; Keith Davies; Ben Edson; Elaine Graham; Liz Henderson; Jan Harney; Lesley Husselbee; Richard Kidd; Michael Lewis; Ian Stubbs; Roger Stubbings; Angela Tilby.

Thank you to the parish of St Peter, Bury, who have not received as much of my time and energy during the writing of this book as they might have justifiably expected, and who have not grumbled – at least to me!

Thank you to commissioning editors at SCM Press: Barbara Laing for encouragement along the way, and to her predecessor, Anna Hardman, for asking me to write the book in the first place.

Thank you, most of all, to Peter, Tilda, Jonty, Theo and

Hugh, Pix and Hubert for being wonderful and showing me so often how grace breaks through.

To Peter, Tilda, Jonty, Theo and Hugh

It is a fearful thing to fall into the hands of the living God.
(Hebrews 10.31)

PREFACE

After I graduated with a degree in ecclesiastical history and divinity from St Andrews University, I went to train as a nurse at the Royal London Hospital in Whitechapel in London: two very different styles of learning, one after another. Lectures, seminars, papers, tutorials and then the experience of the student nurse – working hard on your feet all day (and nights as well) and making the links and connections between necessary practical skills, a knowledge base in drugs and aseptic technique, and, with a developing self-awareness, learning to cope with your reactions to death, birth and everything between. Continually assessed, also, on a range of competencies, from practical skills, like changing a dressing and accuracy in distributing medication, to social and communication skills, bereavement counselling and group dynamics.

Then, when I went to train for church ministry at a residential college, I was puzzled by the lack of any real and explicit attention to developing skills in integrating practice and reflection and self-awareness, especially when residential training resulted in puerile and regressive behaviour at times. It seemed that so much more could have been made of the training as a learning opportunity by making explicit some of the pressures and tensions, and initiating habits of reflection; making stronger connections between the academic, liturgical and worship life and the practical aspects of ministry. But that was in the late 1980s – and much has changed since then (see Chapter 2).

I served my Anglican curacy (a training period of three or

four years working alongside an experienced 'training incumbent' or supervisor) in a town in Lancashire – a good, stretching and fulfilling time. I was lucky. Others of my friends from college had awful experiences. It seemed a very hit-and-miss training experience, and strange that the Church of England traditionally gave so little attention to these extremely important years of curacy in which future ordained ministers continue their training. With little real understanding of the principles of adult education, too often this training has, in the Anglican Church, been left in the hands of senior clergy who might be brilliant at it . . . or not at all. My own training incumbent received, as far as I'm aware, very little in terms of training or support from the diocese. As I say, I was lucky. Neil Burgess's work *Into Deep Water* (1998) tells many other, different stories.

After four years as a curate, I was appointed tutor in Practical Theology at the United Reformed Church (URC) and Congregational Federation college in Manchester, where for a number of years I taught social analysis, political theology and human development, and I was also responsible for the students' (both lay and ordinand) placement learning and the training of supervising ministers. URC ministerial students trained at college for four years, either residentially in college, or else living at home and integrating what they learned on placments in community and church with what they learned through the curriculum offered at college. The selection and training of the supervising minister was taken very seriously by the college staff. Times for reflection were built into college and placement time, using a variety of models of 'doing theology'. To an Anglican working in a Free Church environment, it seemed that what a curate might learn on the job was here being covered in the four years' initial training, for the educational programme was designed to allow for interplay between the contexts of ministry (college, community, home and church), between the different experiences that the students brought, and between different academic studies and the methods of theology. Such cross-fertilization seemed to lay good foundations for students to continue to rate lifelong learning highly.

To further my own skills I trained on a course in supervision and consultation with John Foskett, then chaplain at the South London and Maudsley National Health Care Trust. I subsequently worked alongside him as a tutor on the same course over a number of years. Since taking up my present post as an Anglican vicar I have developed and continue to provide, with Ian Stubbs as a colleague, a course for supervising ministers in the diocese of Manchester. This course runs over ten months of two-hour sessions, and combines reflection on reading and practice (using case studies and verbatim reports as described later in this book) and different methods of theological reflection to support the supervisors in the first year of their colleague's curacy. The methods of this course lie in the Clinical Pastoral Education (CPE) movement, with its emphasis upon understanding the minister, and the situations and people with whom s/he works, as 'living human documents'. This approach, though not without its critics, tends to yield much upon which to reflect and from which to learn.

Theological education is evolving in exciting directions, and skills in supervision and reflective practice are going, I believe, to prove increasingly important. I hope *Lifelong Learning: Theological Education and Supervision* will offer a resource for practice and reflection to theological educators and supervisors alike in the pursuit of lifelong learning.

Frances Ward
Advent Sunday 2004

INTRODUCTION

You find the term 'lifelong learning' all over the place in today's culture, and not just on the notice boards in institutions of further and higher education, in literature on continuing professional education or in books on study skills. Tap the words on an internet search engine and you will gain access to over four million sites. The UK government Department for Education and Skills site will tell you that 'it's never too soon or too late' for learning. The EarlyChildhood site will inform you that lifelong learning starts here. There are courses galore to enhance your skills, to empower the learning community, to 'learndirect', to learn as a family, to learn through transitions, to learn into old age. Lifelong learning, it seems, is everyone's business. The rhetoric has permeated all aspects of life – and church ministry and theological education have not escaped.

The prevalence of lifelong learning indicates a shift of emphasis that has occurred over the last few decades from an understanding of education as something done to you when young, to a sense that education is the responsibility of anyone who takes seriously the need to continue to learn and grow through life, professionally and personally. It is a shift that has happened since John Hull wrote *What Prevents Christian Adults from Learning?* in 1985. There he argued that one of the main problems that faced adult Christians was the traditional understanding of the church as a teaching office that handed on knowledge from teacher to learner. Learning was a passive activity; it was something received. With that view of education, adult learning becomes a contradiction between a return to a childlike state, and the received wisdom that adulthood puts an end to childish ways. To become a learner, as an adult, writes Hull, can be 'to abandon one's adulthood' (1985, p. 208).

Since he wrote in the mid 1980s, learning has become something that adults take responsibility for. You can pick and choose courses that suit your particular needs. Lifelong learning can enable you to gain different skills so that you are able to respond more effectively to a changing work market, or simply enhance your leisure hours. 'Lifelong learning' is so widespread you could be forgiven for thinking that lifelong was the *only* way of learning, and it is important to sustain a range of educational methods, and recognize that for some purposes and at some times of life, different ways of learning are needed.

So who is this book on lifelong learning, supervision and theological education for? It is aimed primarily at those who are training for church ministry in all its many forms, and those responsible for that training, but the book is also for anyone who is interested in reflecting upon their practice. The book offers ways of sustaining the learning and reflection for those who minister, throughout their professional lives. I have used the term 'reflective practitioner' so that the book is inclusive of all who seek to develop through their ministries, whether ordained or lay. By drawing together the current literature on supervision and theological education, I explore what supervision can offer as an *educational* means to sustain adult learning. Supervision is understood here as what happens when a practitioner takes space and time out in an environment that facilitates ongoing processes of reflection on practice. It is facilitated by the 'supervisor', who may work individually with the reflective practitioner, or in a group. In a theological context, supervision can include reflection upon the resources of the living traditions of faith. I suggest that the goal of lifelong learning is the acquiring of practical wisdom in the sense that Aristotle and others after him have used the term 'phronesis' (see Graham, 1996; Flyvbjerg, 2001). The emphasis upon *knowing in action by reflection upon practice* runs through this book as the key goal of lifelong learning.

Hull believes that for this change from teaching to learning to happen, it helps if we use different metaphors and analogies of God: 'as long as the central idea in education was that of teaching, the place of God in a theology of education was clear enough, since he was conceived of as the supreme, all knowing and authoritative teacher' (1985, p. 212). Instead of 'God the teacher', Hull proposes carefully that we understand *God's* nature as one which learns. He writes, 'If we can speak of the adulthood of God, we may say that he is continually renewed through learning, and so is both the ancient of days and the eternal child' (1985, p. 224). In making this proposal, Hull wants to emphasize that the need to learn does not necessarily imply a lack of any sort. It is not something that adults should be ashamed of doing. If God can be understood as a learning God, then we can understand our own learning in the different context of faith in God who is intimately interested and involved in creation, renewed continually by the encounter with the world in an ongoing expansion of life. This book, about lifelong learning, is rooted here. If we can talk of a living God, we can also talk of a learning God, full of loving attention towards the world.

It can be a fearful thing to fall into the hands of a living God. Depending on how God is understood, that fear can be triggered by different things. If God is seen as a strict teacher who cajoles and instructs, who tells us off when we get it wrong, then we will be fearful like some caricature of a Victorian child, vulnerable to a dominant God who is ready to use the ruler when we err. Or it can be a fearful thing to fall into the hands of the living God because God challenges us to learn despite our inclinations not to change, our need to be right, our lack of confidence and our defensiveness. To commit oneself to a process of lifelong learning is to be open to learning throughout life, and from life; from its challenges, failures and possibilities, which will be different at different stages of our lives. To learn means to encounter new experience and other perspectives and this can change us. To learn in the hands of the living God will challenge our sense of identity. It will take us, with a God who is 'both the ancient of days and the eternal child', into a lifelong seeking after understanding that brings us to the limit of our comprehension. As Nicholas Lash says, 'the search for understanding, is for all people and at all times, an *endless* search: whoever you are, and however wise and learned you may be there is always infinitely more that you might try to understand' (2004, p. 8). A lifelong learner is someone who knows there is much more to understand.

This book on lifelong learning is for people who see themselves as engaged upon a journey that is God-given, a journey that seeks God, transcendent and incarnate in the world, a journey of service and ministry. If God is a living God, that journey is a path of life. To be on a path of life is to be willing to be transformed and changed in ways that take us to the core of our identity, where all we hold most dear and most terrifying is found. Learning is to seek after God on a lifelong journey. It is to hope to create ourselves in God's image, as we grow in understanding and in the desire to make a better world. Just as God is both the ancient of days and the eternal child, this journey will not necessarily be a linear one. It may circle around particular areas, familiar or unfamiliar territory, at different times of our lives. If it is a journey of lifelong learning, though, it will be marked by openness to where God leads, a willingness to be changed, a desire to risk former certainties in order to practise faithful discipleship.

An Overview of the Book

Imagine looking down on one of those safety nets provided for high-wire artists at a circus. The net itself is there, primarily, to hold anyone that falls by accident, those who slip or lose their balance. But it gives confidence merely by its presence to those who are competent: it enables risks to be taken high above. And sometimes, imagine, the net is somewhere to dive just for the fun of it; a glorious trampoline where one can bounce and bounce and then lie still and contemplate the wire high above, for a time quiet and swaying gently, with the opportunity to think about new movements, new combinations, different techniques, working relationships. Falling into the hands of the living God is a bit like that, I imagine. It is to fall into hands that hold you, yes, but which also inspire and challenge. The best supervision offers something similar. A holding place of safety, a space that reflective practitioners can rely upon when things go pear-shaped, or when they want to bounce ideas around, or when they need a reassuring sense of confidence. Supervision is a bit like a safety net that offers the security that is necessary for challenging learning to happen.

That safety net requires anchor ropes to suspend it. If supervision is the subject matter of the book, then it can be approached in a number of different ways. I offer seven anchor ropes that give us different ways into the central subject matter – and depending on your approach, you might find it better to read, not from beginning to end, but from a particular chapter that captures your attention.

Anchor Rope One: Learning to Read the Signs of the Times

The literature on supervision has primarily come from a psychotherapeutic background (see Hawkins and Shohet, 2002; Foskett and Lyall, 1990 and the further reading at the end of the book) and as such has offered useful insights to theologians and reflective practitioners. I want, however, to locate the work of supervision more centrally within a learning church and the ministry it offers in today's world. The first anchor rope explores the shape of ministry in contemporary times and the growing impact of globalization upon society. What is it to minister in such a world, and how can supervision support that ministry? The first anchor rope, Chapter 1, locates supervision within the ministry of a church that seeks to serve a changing world.

Anchor Rope Two: What Kind of Learning?

The second anchor rope charts the changes that continue to occur in theological education. It starts with a brief overview of educational theory, noting the influence of writers such as Polanyi, Freire, Kolb and Schön. I then take the developments within the Church of England as a case study, examining the reports from the mid-1980s to the present day as indicative of the way theological education has responded to developments in understanding of how adults learn and integrate their knowledge with practice.

Anchor Rope Three: Learning to Play: The Interplay of Theology

The third anchor rope extends the metaphor of the 'space' that supervision can provide to enable adults to learn. As we explore the space of supervision – that net below us that offers security and confidence to experiment with new practice – I use the work of D.W. Winnicott, his creative approach to playing and reality and his idea of a facilitating environment where learning happens. The space is also seen as the place of encounter, infused by the presence of God, where self and other can engage. We look at the work of John V. Taylor on the go-between God, and others who use Trinitarian theology to provide ways of understanding learning that occurs within encounters with difference, both within ministry and within supervision.

Anchor Rope Four: Learning to Listen: The Practice of Supervision

A fourth anchor rope takes us into the practice of supervision itself and the skilled ability to listen to other people reflecting on their ministry. For listening to happen at any depth, the supervision sessions need to be established clearly in terms of a contract, the working relationship and the context of the organization. Chapter 4 shows how to write verbatim accounts which capture effectively the dialogues of ministry, in order to bring material for reflection on practice. The chapter introduces the 'clinical rhombus', a simple diagram that enables the relationships and dynamics of supervision to be mapped. The phenomenon of the parallel process is explored here. Two verbatim accounts, provided by Sarah and Robert, are worked as examples.

Anchor Rope Five: Learning to Write: The Living Human Document

I draw upon dialogical theory, with its beginnings in the work of Mikhail Bakhtin, to understand further how external and internal dialogues, conversations and other forms of non-verbal communication can be used within supervision. This chapter shows how writing a learning journal can be a form of self-supervision. A journal can provide the tools to consider conversations that occur in ministry and analyse how what is said is often dependent on relations of power between people.

Anchor Rope Six: Learning to Learn: Resistance Good and Bad

Chapter 6 draws us into a consideration of how resistance to learning comes about as powerful emotions of anxiety or fear can inhibit engagement with new material. Resistance to learning usually arises because the learning is hard and there is a desire to avoid it. I give examples of different games that both the reflective practitioner and the supervisor can play to resist learning. This chapter also continues the exploration of how power permeates ministry and supervision. If the supervision that is provided fails to take account of the genuine differences of perspective that the supervised person brings, then it will run into difficulties as the person being supervised will start to resist the learning opportunities that are offered.

Anchor Rope Seven: Learning to Cope with the Downside

Ministry in today's world can be a struggle. This chapter recognizes the need to deal honestly with disappointment and a sense of failure so that, within a learning situation, the reflective practitioner can gain resources to cope with the regret and guilt that can result from mistakes that are made, and the disheartenment and lack of motivation that can result from managing decline within churches.

It may seem that the practice of supervision is addressed directly and properly for the first time in Chapter 4, and if you want to cut to the chase then you can always start to read there. However, there is good reason for the initial chapters: I find it difficult to think about supervision in ministry without thinking about ministry itself in the context of church and world, hence Chapter 1.

Throughout the book I argue that supervision can sustain lifelong learning and that, therefore, it is primarily an *educational* process rather than a *therapeutic* one, and so educational theory needs some exploration as well, particularly the emergence of the notion of reflective practice within theological education.

So we now have a net (Figure 1) that has seven anchor ropes:

1 Learning to Read the Signs of the Times: Ministry in a Changing World
2 What Kind of Learning? Developments within Theological Education
3 Learning to Play: the Interplay of Theology
4 Learning to Listen: the Practice of Supervision
5 Learning to Write a Living Human Document
6 Learning to Learn: Resistances Good and Bad
7 Learning to Cope with the Downside

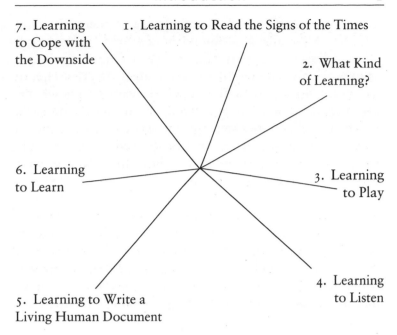

7. Learning to Cope with the Downside

1. Learning to Read the Signs of the Times

2. What Kind of Learning?

6. Learning to Learn

3. Learning to Play

5. Learning to Write a Living Human Document

4. Learning to Listen

Figure 1: The Seven Anchor Ropes.

As it hangs, the net, as seven anchor ropes, would hardly catch anyone, or offer any sort of hammock upon which to swing and reflect. We need some strands that link the anchor ropes. These have been provided by six ministers who were kind enough to write a journal over three days, chronicling their life and ministry. Geoff, Jean, Lynn, James, Ben and Roger wrote for me a full, warts-and-all record that included what they did in their time off, how they felt and what they thought. I wanted a good cross-section of different ministries in the Britain of today. Lynn is a Church of Scotland minister working on a deprived estate in major Scottish city. Jean is a rural advisor in the south of England, with responsibility for a number of Anglican parishes. Geoff ministers in a 'new town', built in the 1950s in a northern city. Ben is a Church Army officer who oversees the development of a fresh expression of church in inner city Manchester called Sanctus1. James is an Anglican curate working in a suburban context in a northern town and Roger is a Methodist superintendent of a circuit in the North West. In asking these particular people, I wanted a range of examples of church life, from rural to inner city, to estate, to new emerging shape of church. Perhaps, on reflection, what is missing is the experience of affluent church-going, though it is there implicitly, for example behind Jean's obvious concern with her engagement with rural issues, and the wealth that lies behind Ben's story of Sanctus1. The experience that each records does, however, raise issues concerning the joys and difficulties of ministry in today's world, and provides the book with cameos of practice upon which to reflect.

Alongside these six strands, three student ministers, Jackie, Sarah and Robert, have also presented us with material from their practice of ministry. We see how Jackie's portfolio works as a way of guided learning and Robert and Sarah have provided verbatim accounts of conversations they had,

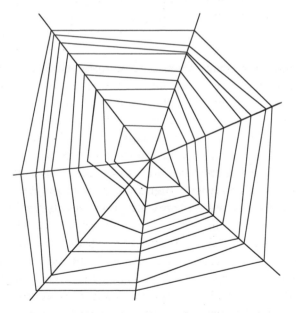

Figure 2: The Seven Anchor Ropes with connecting strands which represent the experience of ministry.

written because the encounters left them with questions that they would bring to supervision.

Drawing was never my strong point! It looks more like a spider's web than a safety net. But then, perhaps as a web it can suggest other ways of thinking about ministry, theological education and supervision. Miller-McLemore has written about 'the living human web' of pastoral practice (1996, p. 9), how we are caught up in many different dynamics which include social forces, personal and political concerns, the whole fabric of institutional life, permeated by power, that make us who we are. Perhaps the 'messiness' of ministry in today's church is better represented by a spider's web, displaying the intricacies and complexities of its delights and disappointments.

Ministry and Supervision in Complex Contexts

In the eyes of many, it is strange to be committed to the ministry of the church in today's world. More often than not, you become part of church and organizational structures that can be bizarre and even frustrating in the way they work. You find yourself working in communities of faith which are complex organisms with hopes and tensions, visions and fears. Ministry is set in the context of day-to-day routines, but it can be unpredictable in the wide range of activities involved. Gone are the days of the lone minister upon whom all depended for the pastoral work and leadership within a pastorate or parish. Now, more often than not, ministry is corporate, agreed with colleagues both lay and ordained, as a community of faith decides upon its visions and priorities for ministry and mission. It can be difficult, though, to assess the effectiveness of ministry. It can be difficult, too, to cope when things get out of control, or when it becomes a business of managing decline. Through a lifelong ministry you can be challenged personally and professionally by an ever-changing church and world that can raise hard issues and confusing questions.

The relationship between the church and the world can seem

a strange one. Is the church there to point the way back to basics, to core values that sustain the fabric of society, promoting the family, honesty in a greedy world, the sanctity of life? Is it there to show the way forward to a more inclusive society where all can discover that they are children of God, find a place and fear no discrimination? What is a church or congregation there to do and be, in a world that seems indifferent; where the foundations of traditional faith are contested and shaken; where many increasingly turn away from institutional and traditional forms of religion towards the appeals of New Age spirituality in the search for well-being and relaxation? How can churches continue to thrive when what Madeleine Bunting (2004) calls 'willing slaves' have no time or energy to offer voluntary organizations like churches, as they did in the past? It can be strange to follow the way, the truth and the life in a society where 'Generation X' and their offspring have little or no residual knowledge about the life, death and ministry of Christ (Lynch, 2002); where competing fundamentalisms seem to be in the ascendancy and the world is an increasingly dangerous place as Christianity, Judaism and Islam fail to live together in peace in many parts of the world.

This book does not attempt to provide any answers to the complexity of church life and ministry in a globalized world. It does seek to explore what ministry is about – the experience of discipleship in the midst of that complexity. It takes seriously the commitment that many people make, and offers some ways in which their lifelong journey can be supported and enhanced by the practice of supervision. It is a book concerned with practical wisdom and adult learning; how adults learn effectively as they reflect critically upon their practice, and find ways to change and enhance who they are and what they do.

How to Use this Book

You can approach this book through a number of entry points, as outlined above. It may be that to start with the six accounts of ministry are a good way to engage – with the reality of their stories. Or perhaps you like to reflect theologically before the rest, in which case Chapter 3 is for you. Wherever you start, though, read this section first which offers some explanation of how to use the book and the key points to grasp.

Turning Life into Text

The six accounts of three days of ministry introduce one of the main ideas of the book. I explore here how personal writing can be used as a means of turning life into text, how 'living human documents' can provide useful material for reflection upon practice. These texts can be professional or personal portfolios, as Jackie shows; or learning journals; verbatim (word-for-word) reports of an encounter in ministry; or a piece of creative writing. Such writing can subsequently be reflected upon either alone in a form of self-supervision, or one-to-one with a supervisor, or within a group. To recognize the importance of texts in this way is to draw on the growing understanding of the place of reflective writing in education and the practice of professional life and continuing ministerial education (see Moon, 2004; Bolton, 2003).

Documents that turn life into text in order to reflect upon practice are an imaginative way of taking forward the Clinical Pastoral Education movement that originated in the United States in the 1920s and 30s with the work of Anton Boisen and Richard Cabot. Cabot pleaded in 1925 'for a Clinical Year in the Course of Theological Study', and in the same year Boisen, recovering from a breakdown, returned to his work as a chaplain at Worcester State Hospital, Massachusetts, and invited some theological students to work with him in the hospital during the summer vacation. He exhorted the theological students to study not only books, but the 'living human documents' (that is, themselves) in pastoral encounters. Allison Stokes writes how 'for him it was an opportunity. How he dealt with this opportunity has affected the course of American religious history' (Stokes, 1985, p. 39). Although

Cabot and Boisen eventually fell out, from their initial collaboration Clinical Pastoral Education (CPE) was born, and
in 1967 the Association for Clinical Pastoral Education was
founded. CPE courses can be found throughout the world,
particularly in the States, but also in Australia, South Africa
and Germany as a mandatory element in theological education to improve the quality of reflective practice by regular
supervision (see the website: www.acpe.edu). There is now a
recently formed UK Association of Clinical Pastoral Education
(UKACPE), which draws together those working and training
in chaplaincy and theological education (for further details,
contact Linda.doyle@slam.nhs.uk). Students work under the
guidance of a qualified supervisor and bring case material
from their ministerial practice to supervision in order to reflect
within a safe and challenging space, either within a group setting or individually. The case material is usually presented in
the form of verbatim reports, and as such are understood as
'living human documents'. This expression captures both the
verbatim record of the conversation that thas occurred in
ministry, and also the practitioner who is presenting the material. As the account is read and performed, for instance, in
role play, the words present the person. This means that the
person can feel that his or her very self is on the line: their life
is being examined, in supervision, like a text.

The expression 'living human document' has been taken
up by many practitioners and practical theologians. Charles
Gerkin, for example, emphasizes the narrative and interpretative elements of the pastoral and learning situation. An
encounter between a counsellor and client becomes a coming
together of the different complex stories of each to create new
interpretations and possibilities for the future. He writes:

When Anton Boisen first suggested that pastors should
include in their preparation 'the study of living human documents,' he proposed an analogy the implications of which
have never been fully developed. Boisen is generally considered the founder of clinical pastoral education in America

and thereby one of the progenitors of the twentieth-century pastoral counseling movement. His concern, however, was only secondarily with pastoral counseling as such. More basic was Boisen's concern that the objectifications of theological language not lose touch in the minds of pastors with the concrete data of human experience. His fear was that the language of theology was being learned by seminarians and pastors without that connection being made. Only the careful and systematic study of the lives of persons struggling with the issues of the spiritual life in the concreteness of their relationships could, in Boisen's view, restore that connection. For Boisen this meant the study of 'living human documents'. (1984, p. 37)

Gerkin highlights Boisen's own concern that theological reflection be integrated with the skills and practice of pastoral counselling. He draws upon the hermeneutical theories of Gadamer and Ricoeur to explore further the way in which the complexities of language and interpretation are present in what he describes as a three-way conversation between 'the Christian tradition, biblical and theological', 'myself and the dilemmas of my life' and 'my counseling practice and its problems'. From a rich interplay between the contributions of each of these points of a triangle (1984, p. 60) an integration of practice and reflection can occur. In ways that Gerkin does not develop, I consider the ways in which learning occurs, on the basis of such 'living human documents', within supervision.

Supervision: What It Is and What It Is Not . . .

I have used the word 'supervision' in this book, but only because it is difficult to find another that describes what we are investigating. At this stage it is perhaps easier to say what it is not. It is different to consultancy, where an expert will, most often at the invitation of a group or individual, come into a situation as an outsider, listen, and offer appropriate guidance. Nor is this book about spiritual direction or guidance, the one-to-one relationship that seeks to understand faith by reflection on prayer and life. Nor is supervision about counselling or therapy, where someone comes for help and healing by talking through difficult situations, thoughts and feelings.

Supervision is about reflection on practice in order to learn to be a more effective practitioner, to be 'a true state, reasoned, and capable of action with regard to things that are good or bad', as Aristotle defined phronesis (quoted in Flyvbjerg, 2001, p. 56). Supervision will often happen when the reflective practitioner is in a training role, but not necessarily: they may be seeking to reflect throughout their learning life under the guidance of someone who can offer a sense of distance from the material under consideration. In training situations, some element of direction and evaluation is necessary; part of the discipline of being trained is accepting that others have the responsibility of oversight of the training and ministry (in this sense of oversight, 'supervision' is the right word). In a training situation appraisal and assessment will be an inevitable part. Appraisal is much more effective, though, when it is integral to learning; when the learner, in collaboration with those responsible for the training process, takes responsibility for the aims and outcomes of his or her own learning. And, of course, anyone in a training or supervisory role is also learning. This book explores methods of supervised reflection that are useful during periods of training, but I recommend that such reflection on practice becomes a habit, a lifelong process that supports continued learning throughout ministry and life.

Identity: Formed in Stone, or Dynamic in Dialogue?

Often theological educators use the word 'formation' to describe the processes of adult learning and preparation for ministry. I do not use the word here, because it suggests to me an end to the process of learning, a formed product as the result, a minister trained and shaped for evermore in some clerical paradigm that values a heroic individualism as a model of ministry. The way the notion of ministerial identity is understood in this book stays with the root of the word 'formation', however. I suggest throughout the book that lifelong learning is about being transformative and 'performative' (Graham, 1996; Atherton, 2003). 'Performative', as Elaine Graham uses the word, means attentive to the ways in which the practices of life and ministry not only reveal faith, but also embody and create faith. So as ministry works at being transformative within the complex local networks of a globalized world, faith communities, Graham argues, perform their faith and, as they do so, they embody the realm of God, a realm of justice and love, peace and hope. Instead of a formed identity as the end result of a training process, lifelong learning is about transforming and performing the living traditions of ministry in today's church and society. It is about embodying the rich inheritance of tradition, scripture, reflective reason and a critical seeking-to-understand the ways of God. In a world of immediacy, of image, of instant communication, the church and its ministry can remind the world of living traditions of hope which are based on a sense of rootedness in life-giving texts and history.

I suggest that to minister is to refuse to understand oneself as ever 'formed', but always open to growth, to the encounter with new ways of doing things and to interpret the given practices and traditions of faith in new ways. It is to see oneself in creative dialogue with others in the world, in dialogue with living traditions of interpreting biblical texts and theological resources from the past, and in dialogue with the present experience of faith in changing cultures. This suggests a sense of identity that is dialogical, willing to share oneself with others and to be open to the (sometimes radical) otherness, or 'alterity', of different viewpoints.

Throughout this book, identity is understood as dialogical and dynamic. Dialogue can be seen to happen in any number of ways and places. First, dialogue is fundamental to all aspects of ministry, whether in face to face encounters, in meetings, by email, in outreach or through networking with different individuals or groups. How and what is said, and what is not said, is significant to the way in which ministry is carried forward. And then as material is brought from the practice of ministry to supervision, dialogue is crucial to the reflection in that secondary situation. If a particular text that is the 'living human document' is brought for consideration, it will contain within it the many different perspectives and voices of the primary situation. The dialogues which occur within supervision can throw light upon the ways in which the minister is engaged in different situations and contexts and in negotiation with others, and can offer the opportunity to experiment with alternative practice.

Then there will be internal dialogues ('Did I really say that?' 'What should I have said then?'), or a constant conversation with someone else that continues in your head after you have left them. To attend to the many ways in which dialogue occurs is to value how it shapes us, how our sense of identity is continuously formed and reformed in encounter and language. To explore a sense of dialogical self is to develop skills and the ability to be reflective and self-reflexive, self-aware and open to learning and reflection upon practice.

To see oneself as dialogical is to attend to one's own voice in different situations. It is to attend to questions of position and power which, I shall argue, permeate all relationships and which needs to be owned and addressed. Michel Foucault's work, especially on the nature of power, has inspired followers to analyse discourse and think further about how language and dialogue involves us in different and complex situations of negotiating power, dominance and authority; the ways in which institutional life can shape and discipline the lives of individuals (see his *Discipline and Punish*, 1975/1991); what it means to the understanding of identity to be in relations of power and difference (see Bernauer and Carrette, 2004). Exploring further that understanding of identity as always in relations of power and difference, I find in the doctrine of the Trinity (Chapter 3) a model of interrelationship and dialogue that provides a pattern of mutuality, of love and respect of difference that can offer rich theological insights into the nature of dialogue.

One of the ways in which dialogue happens is between you, the reader, with your experience of ministry and theological education, and the text of this book. You can make use of the book, and work with the method of reflection upon practice that is used here by writing your own 'living human document' as a learning journal as you read. If you do decide to read the book like this, the activities I have provided will give you the opportunity to pause for thought and to bring what you have read into dialogue with your own experience and thinking. Educationally, this technique is often used in distance learning materials, and can be a helpful way of making the material under consideration your own. This is an option, however. It may be that you prefer to read the book without the interruptions of such 'activities'. If so, simply ignore them.

Activity one

Do you keep a learning journal or a portfolio already? If so, write a side of a sheet of paper describing how you use it – what sort of things you include, how you reflect upon what you have written, how you seek to learn from your experience.

Do you write for someone else – in reality, or in your head? If so, who? And what value do their comments have?

Activity two

George Kelly wrote of Personal Construct Theory in the 1950s (Kelly, 1955). He argued that we construe meaning in our lives and develop constructs that serve as interpretative frameworks (see Chapter 6 below). One of the ways to discover more about your own construct is to write, describing yourself in the third person, as if to a stranger, and explaining the main motivations and passions of your life and ministry.

We turn now to six stories of ministry, six living human documents.

Six Living Human Documents

To think about the practice of supervision and lifelong learning in ministry requires some sense of the realities of church life in today's world. This chapter introduces six excerpts from journals written by ministers who have turned their lives into texts to provide material for reflection. Each gives an account of three days of his or her life, and after each you are invited to engage in dialogue with what they have written, reflecting upon your own situation in the light of what you have read of theirs.

Geoff

I am the Team Rector of a team ministry in a large housing estate on the edge of a major city, having moved to the area about a year before the team became a reality at the end of 1999. The estate, begun in the 1930s but mainly built in the post war years, was intended as a garden city to house people moving out from inner city areas. The five parishes of the team ministry have a population of around 50,000 people. We see being a team ministry as a shared journey in which we are still discovering what it means to be a team, particularly in developing a strategic approach to the problems faced by the churches and the communities which make up the garden city. Whenever new measures of deprivation are published, Wythenshawe's communities always appear among the most deprived in the country, even though there is more and more private development taking place. As a consequence, virtually all of what we do as churches and clergy is influenced by the realities of our social and economic context.

I am now within a few years of retirement, having had

a very varied ministry in and out of the parish context. A housing estate ministry gives no space for a graceful decline, because it requires both hard work and alertness. The alertness is needed because of the steady barrage of vandalism (mostly petty) around the vicarage and the church buildings, and to work with the complexity of the issues which face both community and church, including the very survival of the church into the future.

Sunday

I go round to church at 7.45 a.m. John and Eric always manage to be there before me and have already set up the Lady Chapel altar ready for the 8.30 Eucharist. I prepare for the later service by setting up the amplification system and the digital hymnal which provides music because we have no organist. In between jobs, we stand in the church porch, chatting and greeting people as they arrive for the service.

There are thirteen people, mostly older than me, at the service, which is the Book of Common Prayer service of Holy Communion. At the end of the service I do not have long for greetings and conversation, because I am to preach at the 10 a.m. Eucharist at another church in the team. I arrive there as people are gathering in the Lady Chapel, a triangular space within the main church which is currently unusable whilst the roof is being replaced – at an enormous cost which is, thankfully, being borne by English Heritage. In the Lady Chapel there is a closeness amongst the fifty people present which is very different from being in the main building and there is an immediacy of communication when I preach which is not there when a small congregation is spread across a larger space.

Again I have to leave quickly in order to be back at my own church to preside at the short Eucharist which follows the 10.30 service of Morning Praise. Our Lay Reader has led and preached at this service; there seems not to have been a large congregation, though a fair number remain for the Eucharist. Ours is the only church in the team to still have an early service of Holy Communion but it divides the worshipping community into two unequal halves. The morning ends as I help to clear up and chat with the people who are on duty in the vestry. Then it is home to eat some lunch, fall asleep for a while, and then spend some time on administration. Since we rarely have evening worship of any kind, the evening is mine to enjoy with friends.

Monday

I walk down to the local shop to buy a newspaper, since the shop recently gave up delivering papers. I enjoy the outing, exchanging greetings with several people and a snatch of conversation with one or two. Both Monday and Tuesday have more than enough meetings, but first I need to see the doctor about some niggling aches and pains in my arm and shoulder. He speaks of arthritis and sends me for X-rays at the hospital.

I am now late for my meeting with Daphne, a member of the Methodist Church. Once a month we share our main service with the Methodist and United Reformed churches. Daphne and I are one of three teams which take turns to lead this united worship; we are to begin planning the November service, which will be on Remembrance Sunday. We work quickly and easily. We soon have an outline and a basic theme and fix a date for a meeting at which we will finalize the service.

Back at home I have a short time to sit at the computer and work on some grant applications which I am completing for Thursday's meeting of a group which is trying to establish an ecumenical community work project. This is to help the churches to engage better with community issues, to create partnerships with other groups and agencies, and to bring some coherence to our separate efforts. Despite some interruptions (the phone and a caller at the door wanting food) I make some progress.

I hurry my lunch so as to be on time at the first meeting of a working party of a local community network. We are concerned at what we see as the failure to involve the community in planning the reshaping of services which will follow the ending, next year, of the local partnership body and the Single Regeneration Budget. We bounce thoughts and ideas off each other and plan two more meetings to complete the paper we want to produce. Whether we can actually influence either the consultation process as already determined or its outcome remains to be seen. There is a massive gap between local authority processes and the way in which people relate to what is going on in their community – or at any rate that is how we see it.

I have a little space when I return home and use it to catch up on telephone and email messages, to think about the evening's meeting, and to read the newspaper. I even manage to prepare and eat my evening meal in good time to set out for the meeting of the Team Council.

Before the meeting we have a Eucharist to keep St Michael's and All Angels Day. Once the meeting begins we are plunged into a mix of major and minor matters. We spend most time on one thorny matter. This is the pastoral care and development of the one parish in the team which does not have a team vicar and which before long will not have a member of the clergy team living in it and leading its development. We decide to set up a discussion between that church's council and the Team Council. We do not manage to complete the agenda for the meeting, but I sense that we have grappled with real and difficult issues concerned with the future direction of the team ministry.

Tuesday

The clergy team meets for worship every Tuesday morning. Though we only have a formal meeting once a month, we often spend up to an hour after worship, chatting and sharing news and doing some business over coffee. There are seven of us at present, as many as we are ever likely to be, including two curates. I drag myself away to join briefly a meeting between the regional organizer and the senior officer of the local branch of Home-Start which I chair. We discuss staffing matters and then I leave them for the final meeting of the morning which is with one of our team to discuss some problems arising from the report on a community audit which was carried out some months earlier.

Back in the parish after lunch, there is a meeting of an ecumenical study group. It has been meeting over the past year, and we need to decide whether and how we should continue into the future. I am concerned that the group should actually help to resource us for mission and outreach; I am wary of the commitment this might require from me. However, people are eager to continue, and we decide what material we will use and that we will meet four times through October to December.

After two brief pastoral visits I now have the evening to eat my meal at leisure, spend some time with the Brownies and Guides (or at any rate with their leaders), and give some more attention to the community work project and the grant applications connected with it.

As you read through Geoff's account, what would you say are the main motivations and passions of his ministry? How are they different from or similar to your own?

Jean

No three days are ever the same but that's what I like about being in rural ministry. Right now I minister in five rural churches in deepest Dorset and am the Rural Officer for the Churches in Dorset. There is never a dull moment! Last night I attended a wonderful carol service in the nearby town to celebrate the support given to our local Women's Refuge. We are told that one in four marriages experiences some form of domestic violence so clearly we are only helping a very small proportion. Our benefice of churches has adopted the refuge as its charity. We make collections of useful things like sheets, towels, cleaning materials and Christmas gifts and raise additional funding for them through our barn dance, Lent lunches and carol services. It was good to meet other supporters of the project and for once not to have to lead the service!

Morning prayer in the nearest church is always a good start to Monday and attracts a regular congregation. I am able to discuss our forthcoming Advent Quiet Day with one of my Reader colleagues before driving into town. There I have been meeting with local Agenda 21 activists and those who are buyers of food for public bodies like hospitals, schools and care homes. It is amazing how much food is transported much further than it needs to be and we are campaigning for more local produce to be used by public bodies. Not only will this be beneficial to the environment by reducing food miles but it will help support farming businesses, many of which are struggling at the present time. On the way home I visit a parishioner in the hospice. I have lunch in a local pub with a member of Farm Crisis Network (FCN) who has come to interview a farming family in the county that has applied for help with housing from the ARC-Addington Fund. Housing tied to the job is a rather mixed blessing when redundancy comes along. In the afternoon, I meet with our benefice lay pastoral assistants who undertake parish and hospital visiting and then I have time to catch up on emails and phone messages. My secretary comes tomorrow so the final task of the day is to plan next weekend's worship so that she can prepare whatever we need in printed form.

Next day finds me driving over into Somerset for a meeting

on rural housing needs. Present are rural housing enablers, County and District Councillors and planners of all kinds. I represent the churches on the South-West Rural Affairs Forum and get invited to many such seminars on various topics. I have to be selective but affordable rural housing is high on the churches' agenda too. Later I'll arrange to meet with our Diocesan Property Agent with a view to determining whether we may have some land suitable for use in meeting housing needs. I return via the Dorset College of the Countryside where I am a member of the governing body. We are preparing for an Ofsted (Office for Standards in Education) inspection in 10 weeks' time. The meeting is relatively speedy, all the inspection needs seem to be coming together and I am able to get away in time to join the local NFU branch for their AGM. They have asked me to say something about the housing scheme for farming people. Several of my own parishioners are there and there is time to catch up on their news. One of the local NFU members is keen to get support for a trip to blockade the dairies who are not paying a realistic price for milk. Most of the Dorset farmers are currently paid less for their milk than it costs them to produce and they need another 2p a litre to make a living. I wonder whether I should join them on the picket lines. The Diocese has just become a fair trade zone and this should surely apply to our own dairy farmers as to the tea and coffee producers in East Africa. In the end I decide that 4 a.m. on the picket lines would not be good news for my day job but I shall be with them in prayer and in spirit. All I can personally do is buy my locally produced milk in the village shop. At the end of the evening, the County FCN coordinator reminds me that it may be time for us to renew our request to the Health Authority for funding on the basis that our FCN help line has a preventive role.

My day off dawns bright and cold. I spend some relaxing time in the garden away from the phone and trying to catch up on autumn tasks. My hens are still laying eggs almost as well as they did in the summer months. I am glad of them since the aim for the afternoon is to make one layer of a wedding cake for our daughter's wedding next year. Once that cake is in the oven I am off to the shops. I resist the temptation to answer the phone on my day off, but I call our County Councillor who wants to talk about the need for a Day Centre in one of our villages. I persuade him that we should plan to use paid and trained workers to run such a centre, if we are able to get it started. There are many folk living alone and regular outings to a Day Centre would I think improve the quality of life for many of them. I try hard to shop well ahead for most things to say nothing of Christmas and currently I am feeling a bit behind schedule. Living so far from big shops means that I try to shop when I need to travel and next weekend will be a good opportunity for I am going up to London for the AGM of WATCH (Women and the Church, a campaigning group in the Church of England working towards equality of women in ministry). On the way back from today's shopping I visit a Woodland Burial Ground which at present is little more than a ploughed field. Such sites seem to be in demand and I have two or three churchyards which may lend themselves to limited versions. It would be worth finding out what the issues are before I suggest the idea as I have found that some people have fairly fixed ideas about churchyard management. I am responsible for five open churchyards and they do create quite a bit of work at times. In the evening, I am able to get into the sewing room for a while and progress one or two long overdue projects. Sub-consciously I am preparing the next morning's school assembly!

Jean's account reveals a complex interplay between her community engagement in her role as rural advisor and her ministry in the different parishes she serves.

Draw a diagram of the different roles you hold, professional and personal. How do you manage potential conflicts between the different roles?

Roger

My entire ministry, since I began in 1977, has been in the north-west of England: in Leyland, Fleetwood, Crosby, Horwich and now Salford, where I have been serving as Superintendent Minister of the Salford Methodist Circuit since it came into existence following the amalgamation of two circuits in 2003. In many ways the appointments have been quite similar: small towns on the edge of larger towns or cities. The latest appointment has brought the greatest responsibilities, not least when the amalgamation of the two circuits doubled the number of churches and the number of colleagues on the staff team. I have seven years to the normal retirement age of sixty-five.

Friday

I start this three-day diary on the Friday evening with a particularly happy event. A drive up to Leyland to be present at the Welcome Service for the new minister there who was a teenager at the church I served in Crosby brought back happy memories as he had kindly invited me to be the Assisting Minister at his ordination back in 1998. An excellent sermon by the Chair of the North Lancashire District was an added bonus. The beginning of September in Methodism marks the beginning of a new church year with the round of church meetings and activities starting up again after the summer lull. For me it has been a busier summer than normal. Early in the year it became likely that a colleague who would be moving this year would not be replaced because of the shortage of ministers available. This led to the need to spread the present ministers more thinly to close the gap. Then, during the period when the Methodist Conference was in session at the end of June, within just a few days three ministers were offered to us and there was the need for several hastily convened meetings of the Circuit Leadership Team to consider each possibility with only a day or two each time to think through the issues involved. In the end there was what looks to be a good outcome, but the experience was an exhausting one for all concerned.

As I approached the beginning of September, I found myself being overwhelmed by all that seemed to be facing me as I looked in the diary, and a period of depression had descended. So it was good to be at this service tonight to be reminded through past connections that my ministry had had some significant effect on other people! And so I drove home in a much more buoyant mood, home early enough to put things on my desk for what was to be an unusually busy weekend ahead.

Saturday

Up and away soon after 9 a.m. to get to our Worsley Road church for the Circuit Policy Review Day which was to begin at 10 am and end at 3.30 p.m. Three of us on the planning group and there is always apprehension as to how such a day will pan out and whether it will do what we hope. I had struggled to get thoughts on paper for the two bits of input I was due to give. In many ways I see myself more as a pragmatic person than a great visionary. I need not have worried; our District Mission Enabler led an excellent opening session on the nature of the church in Britain today. Things just went on from there and the time flew by. The general consensus seemed to be that it had been a good and useful day and gave much food for thought. The important thing now is for us to collate the insights that we gained and bring a realistic and practical action plan to the Circuit Meeting later this month. The only criticism that I have heard about the day came the next day when someone said they were disappointed that we hadn't worked on an action plan at the meeting itself as they feared the momentum would be lost. I said that I had felt we should distil what we had learned through the exercise first, but realized I was being somewhat defensive in my reply.

Nevertheless I went home and felt good; the first part of a

busy weekend was behind and that was a load off my mind.
This evening I drove in warm sunny weather through the
countryside of East Lancashire to the Welcome Service in
Great Harwood for the colleague who moved there at the
beginning of August. It was good to be able to wish him
well at the refreshments that followed and to have interesting chats with several people, not least a fascinating conversation with his future Anglican colleague about Bishops of
Blackburn past and present!

Sunday

This was to be an unusually full day. The time for my own
prayers was somewhat truncated this morning, but I did manage to pray for all the preachers in all our thirteen churches,
which I always try to do on Sunday morning. Then it was off
to The Height Church as it was my turn on the rota to preside at the monthly 9 a.m. Communion, with one of my colleagues giving a short homily. I had decided to use a printed
liturgy I have in stock from the Church of South India. It
made a refreshing change and seemed to be appreciated. The
events of the tragic ending to the school siege in Beslan, Russia were much in people's minds and I had decided to include
in both services this morning something that might help us
express our solidarity with the grief of those we had seen on
our television screens. Before I entered the ministry I taught
modern languages. So we stood for the Lord's Prayer which
I said in Russian first, after which we all said it in English.
It was moving and appreciated, it seemed, by the congregation. After the service there was the usual breakfast: a short,
happy time of fellowship and news from around the circuit.

Then I drove the short distance to Manchester Road church
for their 10.45 a.m. service. There the congregation, like
many, struggle with an ageing building, there is no organist
or pianist for the hymns, but it is in such churches that I often
find such hopeful faith. They have an excellent mini-disc system that provides organ accompaniment for the hymns, a

small working group had given a much-needed repaint to some of the rooms; the table at the back of church always has up-to-date literature and an attractive church newsletter. There is optimism in what could be a depressing environment, and that optimism is infectious; leading worship there is a joy.

After several conversations at the end of the service, it was time to come home and get lunch, watch a bit of television at the same time before an afternoon meeting with the church stewards of my larger church. A photo-call preceded the meeting, as at the annual meeting in May someone relatively new to the church said they didn't know who was who amongst the church officials. We have a good team and there is fun as well as business. At the July Church Council we had included an exercise 'What Do We Expect of Our Minister?' and I was able to share with them the results of the poll and reflect with them on the demands of the last year with regard to leading worship, administration, teaching and visiting. I shared with the group what I perceived as my own strengths and particular interests and a useful and affirming discussion ensued. Again this was something I needed at this particular time when I had been looking ahead in my diary and feeling more and more overwhelmed by everything that was awaiting me.

When everyone left I felt guilty that I had not called on a church member yesterday who is in the Acute Stroke Unit of the local hospital. He was not expected to pull through when he was taken ill suddenly at the beginning of the week and I had called in every day to spend some time with him and his wife who was at his bedside. Amazingly he has survived, though the long-term future is far from encouraging. I decided to call to see his wife, who would be home from the hospital. She was actually surprised that I had said I would come to the hospital yesterday, as she knew what a busy day it was. Another example of my need to be realistic with the time available and the tasks to be fitted into that time!

A bite to eat before setting off to Rixton, for the service that was to mark the transfer of that church from our Circuit to the Warrington Circuit. The Chair of the Liverpool District and our own Deputy Chair of District were present and there was a full church on a hot night. The worship was celebratory, though tinged with the sadness of farewells to the folk in that church where one had preached often.

It was good to get home and to sit, read and listen to music.

Monday

Monday morning is seldom my best time, but the first Toddlers Service of the new year, with their percussion and action songs, was first thing on my list after breakfast and prayers. Unfortunately the rest of the morning was full of frustration. My internet connection failed on Saturday evening and this always causes me angst! So there was some time on the phone with the maker's helpline to see if it was the modem which was at fault. A lot of moving the computer to different sockets and using different cables eventually solved the problem and most of the morning was gone. To cap it all I look out of the back window and what I thought was to be a gentle pruning of the trees in the manse garden that had grown again the church wall, was in the process of becoming a decimation of all the greenery that sheltered the manse from the church. Psychologically, that greenery had been helpful to give me the impression that I was not really living over the shop. Sadly it was too late to remedy the situation and I shall have to think of some quick-growing bushes for next year.

As always I was looking forward to my day off the next day, Tuesday, and the rest and relaxation it will bring, so I called a former teaching colleague whom I'd not seen for twenty-five years and arranged to visit him in the south of the Lake District.

After lunch there was the final preparation for an evening meeting and then the short drive to the hospital to spend a few minutes sitting with the church member and his wife.

By then it was time to head back home for tea and a little time dealing with the emails that had stacked up while I
was offline. The secretary of the committee that was to meet
rang to ask if she could come and see me before the meeting.
As always in such cases, I wondered if she was coming to
hand in her resignation. But in the eventuality it was to share
an anxiety that she hadn't been informed about something
between meetings and she needed to express her annoyance
to someone. We parted friends.

As a circuit superintendent, Roger has to be concerned
about a shortage of ministers within his circuit and having 'to close the gap', although in this circumstance there
was a last minute reprieve as the Methodist Conference
sent three ministers at the last minute.

Many denominations face a growing shortage of
stipendiary ministers. How does this impact upon your
ministry and the church in your locality as you look
towards the future?

Lynn

When I went to be minister in my first charge I was handed
a copy of the congregational roll bearing the names of 565
members and a pile of black and white photographs. The
photographs were pictures of the past glories of the church.
Among pictures of a large group of young women I recognized many of the now much smaller Guild who are now con-
siderably older. Pictures too of a huge company of the Boys'
Brigade who have dwindled to a handful of boys. At 26 I was
the minister of a church whose previously huge organizations had shrunk. All that remained of those days of growth
in the Sunday school, the choir, the youth fellowship and
the other church organizations were these black and white
photographs. I inherited a church run by the people who
had been there and who wanted to return to numbers and
strength. I perceive it now as a church whose roots were in

modernism and looked to its organizations and its structures to bring new life into its walls.

After ten years I moved to Millhill,[1] situated in an area of multiple deprivations on the other side of the city. Perhaps it shouldn't have come as a surprise when I was handed a roll with 139 names and a pile of black and white photographs which were suspiciously familiar. Same organizations, albeit slightly smaller numbers and different faces. The difference this time was that the remnant was almost non-existent. There were four boys in the Boys' Brigade, five in the Guild, no choir, no permanent musician, eight in the Sunday school (swollen at that time by a family of six) and no other youth work in the Church.

The major difference was that the church no longer felt that their organizations could be revived. The structure of Congregational Board and Kirk Session which exists to run and lead the church was also full of unfilled posts and undone tasks. There was no pressure to restore what had been and instead this small church had a grandiose plan to change the church into a theatre and a café in conjunction with the local arts group. The plan was old by the time I arrived and the arts group were no longer interested, but there was still a feeling of 'try anything and if it doesn't work we were expecting not to be here anyway'. I have to admit to feeling of 'What have I done?' as I imagined myself battling on as the twenty or so worshippers gradually diminished before my eyes. As it was, that didn't happen, due more to the people and my project worker than to me.

We started a food co-operative and a café which is staffed by paid workers. We took every opportunity to let or use the building or offer a service. So we now give space to a furniture store run by the local mission, a meeting of home helps on a Tuesday, a carers' group and a pick-up point for the local credit union. As well as these things we run lunch clubs,

---

[1] The story of this congregation has been told and analysed by Will Storrar in *Studying Local Churches: A Handbook* (edited by Helen Cameron, and others, SCM Press, 2005).

nearly-new stalls, outside catering and a milk token scheme. It seems a lot but perhaps a run through the week will tell you a bit about what we don't have as well.

Sunday

Get to church to open up around 10 a.m. as we don't have a church officer. Then go to pick up two of our older members. Very few of us have cars and those who do are always running around picking people up. One of these ladies will organize tea and coffee for after the service as she has done for years and years and she brings with her the home-made cake as she has always done. She is 86. Jean, the Church of Scotland project worker, has arrived before I get back to the church and she has let in the lady who comes early to 'be on the front door'. Jean was not part of the church when I arrived. She came after her younger son was killed in a motorcycle accident. There are about 45 people at worship. We are ordaining new elders. The congregation still think it is funny that when it was announced that we were ordaining new elders, one of them said 'Is that for the tree?' (We have a copper tree in the church in the memorial chapel where people can put a leaf inscribed with the name of someone who has died.) This remark was met with puzzlement until she said, 'Are the welders coming for the tree?' The banter then continued as they mused as to whether or not in our situation welders might not be better than elders: young men or even men in the church and useful ones at that. Our guitarist accompanies the singing and the worship is as always punctuated by people going out to the toilet, today joined by one who is heavily pregnant. This raises a bit of concern when she is away a long time, so someone goes to check on her.

After the service I see a couple about a wedding and then go back through to the café to join in the food that the café staff has prepared so that we can celebrate our new elders. Then we make arrangements to run everyone home. Then I take my eight-month-old golden retriever round to Jean's house where we have a snack lunch and he plays with her rottweiler. Sometimes we will go out on a Sunday but today I have to go home and prepare for a 4.30 p.m. service for the Week of Prayer for Christian Unity at the nearby Catholic chapel. We are well supported by our friends from the Roman Catholic church across the road but there are only a handful of people at worship.

There is no such thing as a normal week at Millhill. I suppose all ministers would say something like that about their church but I feel I have to start here because it feels like a defining statement within our work. Jean and I are constantly saying that we haven't done very much on a particular day, but that usually means we haven't done what we intended at the beginning of the day. Our situation is an important contributory factor. We work from the church and are based in an office in the middle of the building. On one side are the hall and the café and on the other side are the church and our child bereavement project which is called Millhill's Hope.

Monday

We start on a Monday at 9 a.m. after Jean and I have walked our dogs in the local park. I mention this because sometimes we start talking about work at 8.30 a.m. as we are walking the dogs. On other days we start in the café with a coffee with the staff and sometimes with the staff of Millhill's Hope. It is a pleasant start to the day but a quick way of catching up on work and local gossip. Today we find out that the administrative assistant's sister has had a baby daughter and that things are being stolen from the houses that are awaiting renovation. Moving to the office we have a weekly planning meeting with Alison, the manager of Millhill's Hope. Jean manages the development of the projects and we are both members of the management committee of Millhill's Hope and it is in this capacity that we meet with Alice to provide support and supervision. Alice tells us this morning of a family who has raised a particular issue for her. It seems that whilst she was assessing the family to see if the children would benefit from coming to Millhill's Hope she was told that their parent had died of heart failure. Sometime later it emerged that it was in fact suicide. The project believes that it is important for children to know the truth about what has happened to their relative and will not usually begin work if this is not the case. In this situation, however, work had already begun with the children before Alice became aware that she had not been told the truth. We spent much of our time discussing to what extent truth was necessary for the child to benefit from the project.

Jean and I then met to discuss the café and all the other activities that take place in the church and its hall. The work was then divided up for the morning. The community deacon joined us for part of the meeting. Whilst these meetings sound smooth we are continually interrupted by phone calls and by people coming up from the café. We have volunteers running a furniture store and others a second-hand clothes stall on a Monday, Wednesday and Friday. They all feel at home coming in and out of our room if they have a question or a problem. Very few of our volunteers disturb us unless there is a something that they need to ask. Similarly we have a phone connection to the café and we often take calls which need to be transferred so that someone can speak to the staff or even someone who is sitting in the café. Sometimes life is made up of hundreds of two minute jobs. We have often tried to find another way but it keeps us very much part of all that is going on and helps our volunteers especially to feel supported. The morning passes and then the accountant phones saying he has emailed a set of accounts that need to be checked and returned to him for the next day. These are the accounts for the projects. Jean and I are both involved in trying to do the administrative work that goes with the café and church and supporting the administrative assistant in Millhill's Hope. Neither of us want to do as much of this work but again it is hard to see how else it can be. We have very few people in the church who work and even fewer who have skills in administration. Things like insurance, data protection, health and hygiene, child protection, café money, food co-operative money, applying for grants and dealing with other agencies can easily fill a day if not a week. I should mention that I am also property convener for the church because we have no one who can take this on at the moment. Monday is gone and Tuesday comes along.

Tuesday

Tuesday is the kind of day that I like. Still on the admin that runs through the week, in the morning I am interrupted. The café staff phone up to say that there is a couple who have come in to see if I can marry them. They are too polite. I know there is something else. I go down to the café and find that she is in her forties and he is in his late seventies. I take them up to the only quiet room in the church (it used to be my vestry, but is now a room for the counsellor who helps Millhill's Hope). This is our parish, they say, and they are having their reception at the local pub which is frequented by long-term alcoholics. They have fallen out with most of both of their families. She is disabled and he is her carer. They want to get married in the church because she has never been married before and it has been a lifelong dream. She wants to know what she will do with the large black bag that she always carries because she doesn't like to be parted from it for long. Alcohol is a major factor in all that they are but I am sure that they both want this ceremony. It is six weeks from now and they need an answer. Agreeing to marry them is not difficult for me as I have been in similar situations so often before and have thought it through. They have come to the café but this is the first time in decades that they have been near the church. A refusal will destroy the frail bridge they have crossed and for me this is always a potential beginning. They will make the effort to come on a Sunday before they get married, they say. That will be a huge step for them. 'Don't drink before you come', I suggest, and they say they won't. I believe it is better than shutting the door. We will meet and talk again before the day.

They are followed fairly soon afterwards by a couple with a young child. They want their two children baptized. I have never met them before. She is quiet. He is the one who wants the baptism. He was brought up a Catholic and even thought of being a priest. He is in the army and home on leave. He is straightforward like most of the people in Niddrie. He tells me he doesn't believe in coming to church but this baptism is important to him. We have a wide-ranging good-humoured discussion where I try to find out exactly what he is saying. He starts with lots of criticisms emanating I think from a very strict Catholic upbringing. I sympathize but I also point to much that is positive in the Catholic Church and I say that at times we haven't been much better. He brings up his difficulties with Adam and Eve, the Ascension, a padre in the army who passed out leaflets asking what you would do if you were to die today just before they went into battle, a comrade who died, a prayer that wasn't answered and his theory that God might have been an alien! We discussed them all. I asked his wife if he ever let her get a word in edgeways. She laughed and he continued talking. I asked her what she felt and she said she could not take the vows as I had explained them. He said he could not promise to come to worship but he kept saying, 'I'm just being honest.' So we kept going on the theme of honesty and eventually admitted that he talked for Scotland but beyond all the talk was a faith that was important to him. I talked a bit about church as a place where questions are raised and explored and where the community need a chance to know the children and to love the children when they take a vow. He agreed to come and he came the following week. I wish sometimes that we had spent more time on things like apologetics and how relevant our churches are to people's explorations in faith.

In the café and with all its goings-on, the kind of discussion that I had with him is usually slowed down and only covers one topic at a time. In the same week one of the folk in the café produces a magazine where the resident clairvoyant is answering a letter that is clearly from one of the people in the parish whose son choked to death in his room. He had locked the door. The people are all impressed by the detail in her answer. Four or five of us have a long discussion about clairvoyance and Christianity. I always have something else to do when these discussions start but they seem to be at the heart of what the café is about.

During the week I do get out to schools and to do a little visiting. My neighbour has died and that is the only funeral. The rest of the time I am in the church. I know from reflection on my last parish that it is a different model of ministry. Sometimes my involvement is very practical as when we help a social worker or health visitor with clothes or furniture. A health visitor comes in this week because she is working with a woman with mental health problems and drug misuse. She has a new house but little furniture and no food or money. This is becoming increasingly common. Social workers are inundated and they send people to us. The volunteers look to me or Jean to become involved in the decision as to what we give and whether we can give any other kind of support. We never give money but we do occasionally allow a free dinner from the café particularly when, as with this woman, there are young children in the house. My project worker and I are having a go at working a forty-hour week. At the end of the week I am pleased because I am just a couple of hours over but it has been easier than some weeks. Next week will be different. It may be about a parent from Millhill's Hope or a management committee meeting or a problem for one of our volunteers or we just need to go to the cash-and-carry for the café or something else. None of these happened this week, but it's anyone's guess what happens next week.

Lynn's ministry at Millhill centres predominantly within the church plant with its many projects and community activities. How is your church building used? What are the places and spaces in which your ministry is located?

James

I am the curate of a small Anglican church. At the time of writing my training incumbent is on sabbatical. We have an approximate Sunday attendance of fifty, slap bang in the middle of a large run-down council estate. Recently we came out top in the crime statistics of Greater Manchester, and the area is probably best described as desolate, with most of the problems being behind closed doors. I live with my wife and daughter in one of the council houses further into the estate. I've only been a curate for two years and it's been a steep learning curve, but exciting! The church is hugely involved in work with asylum seekers, and works closely with a number of other churches in the area, including a New Testament Church of God, a Methodist church, an Independent Methodist church and another Anglican church. In the two years I've been here we've had to close one church building and unite two separate church congregations, which has been painful for all concerned. The area has also seen a massive growth in the Asian community which has led to much ill-feeling amongst the white community. The church building is located between a huge new mosque and a Hindu temple.

Sunday

I arrive at church just after 7.30 a.m. It's been a long night. We had a homeless guy call at the door at 10 p.m. He attends the church on a Sunday so we know him well, but he was hungry and pretty fed up with life on the streets. It was a really tough decision, because we've had people sleep on the sofa before, but this time we decided it was safest not to let him sleep in the house, because of our little one. We gave him some food, and put him in our hammock in our back garden with a blanket to keep him warm and dry. Not ideal, but all we could safely do at the last minute. But it meant a restless night worrying about him, thinking if we should have had him in the house.

Our morning service kicks off at 10.30 a.m. but because we meet in a slightly posh version of a church hall there's a whole sound system to set up, chairs to arrange, music to get ready, and a million and one things to get organized. This morning was particularly chaotic. A brother and sister decided to have a fight before the service so I had to remove them from the building. It wasn't the most prayerful beginning to an act of worship, but it was certainly 'alternative'. The churchwardens arrived about 9.30 a.m. and helped get ready for the service.

Services are probably the most stressful time for me personally. Today I lead the service, preach, preside over Communion, and lead the music on my guitar, which means having to be prepared well, like a military operation, but also means that I leave the service and church at about 12.30 p.m. after coffee and the clearing away of the church, not sure whether I've actually found the space personally to be aware of God at all. This is not always the case, but not uncommon.

Coffee after the service is always an adventure. Its always a toss up between spreading yourself thin by running around everyone saying hello, or getting into deep conversation with some of our members who have issues they want to discuss. We have quite a high proportion of people who suffer from mild to some quite severe mental health problems, so coffee time can be a quite draining, but an incredibly rewarding time. Today is quiet and people want to get home to watch the Olympics.

Sunday lunch is fantastic. Quiet, restful, and we just sit and read the Sunday newspapers.

In the afternoon I take my daughter swimming at our gym, which she loves, and I do some training at the gym for an hour. In the evening I go to a service at the church up the road because we have no evening service.

I spend a little bit of the evening getting ready for the week ahead, thinking through things to do, people to visit. And a little time in the evening, thinking about the morning service. It's frustrating to see a church losing people and not knowing why. We're trying very hard to make our services user-friendly and accessible, sermons interesting and the church very involved in the community, but we still seem to be struggling to make any impact.

Monday

Start work about 8 a.m. setting up the church website and the notice sheet so that I'm ready to print it for Sunday. I leave it ready for amendments during the week, but get the majority of it finished. Write an article for the parish magazine which is guaranteed to put people to sleep, but the best I can do. Read the Bible readings for next Sunday so that I can spend the week thinking/praying them over ready for sermon writing on Friday. Send some emails; get interrupted by a knock at the door, and spend about 20 minutes chatting and feeding another guy off the streets. Make a few phone calls and basically spend the morning catching up on paperwork.

Today's paperwork consists of filling in an application for money from the Youth Evangelism Fund for a community project I'm organizing with the local housing association. As a result of the decline of the estate I was invited onto a panel that wants to renovate the whole estate, but they have neither the funding nor the people to do it. So I'm organizing a pilot project to renovate a small area of the estate, with new gardens, fencing, cleaned of graffiti, and making the area look and feel a lot better. The idea is to use the lads who've been causing the trouble, to undo the damage they've done. But getting funding from the Church is not proving very easy. I'll say no more! I'm rubbish at filling in forms and we've videoed interviews with the kids on the estate talking about the project which I've spent a little time trying to edit, but with no success. Some of the words used in the video won't really help the application, if you catch my drift!

Monday lunch is always a fixed 'date' with my wife. While my daughter sleeps we have lunch together and pray together. It doesn't always happen but we try to defend it as sacred time, both because it's great to eat together, and because it's the main time we pray together. Today however our daughter wakes up so it's a prayer triplet rather than the two of us.

I spend the afternoon studying. Part of my agreement with my incumbent is that I have one afternoon a week to carry on with study. At the moment I'm reading Dallas Willard's *The Divine Conspiracy* and I'm about to start an MA at the Nazarene Theological College, so I spend a little time looking through their prospectus. I pop out to buy a book for a church member who wants to give a suitable book to a non-Christian friend.

I spend most of the evening with my wife, but make a couple of phone calls: one to sort out the sound system at church and the other dealing with a preaching date for the next door parish. They haven't got a minister at the moment.

Tuesday

We're trying to help an asylum seeker find a lawyer, which is nearly an impossible task. I make a few phone calls early on to try and help this person, but get nowhere. This is quite a common occurrence, although normally my incumbent deals with this side of parish ministry.

Mid-morning I take a Communion service at a local retirement home, having walked down the road to pick up my *Daily Mirror* (the best newspaper around), a can of energy drink, and a chocolate bar. A long day's work needs a balanced diet!

Just before lunch I take the video camera I've borrowed from a local youth project back so that they can use it to film a community project they're doing. I chat to the youth worker there for half an hour and then come home for lunch, just in time to say hello to my daughter before her lunchtime sleep.

This morning I had in my diary to visit two old ladies who are in hospital at the moment. I just haven't been able to pop in, which I'm a bit annoyed about because I find having time to visit difficult at the best of times, and so to miss an opportunity makes things difficult for the rest of the week.

Straight after lunch I have a meeting with the boss of the housing in the area. We spend about an hour and a half walking around the estate looking at areas she would like to see renovated and we talk about the role of the church in helping change the community. She is in the middle of dealing with some Anti-Social Behaviour Orders and we talk about the consequences of that. I find it really frustrating because for the first time in a while the community and the local authorities are crying out, literally, for the church to help. It is a great opportunity, but we have so few people and resources to help that I feel like my hands are tied. But I come away from the meeting encouraged that perhaps there are some small inroads being made by the church, and by the work I'm trying to build.

Grab a cup of coffee on the run, and head up to a local youth project and spend the rest of the afternoon just eating biscuits, chatting to kids who are involved in petty crime and drugs. It's probably the best thing I've got involved in since arriving on the estate. It's given me an inroad into the lives of many families, and also given me the pulse of the estate. If I get anything pinched, the youth project inhabitants will soon find out who did it and get the stuff back for me! I tend to work closely with one of the youth workers who has recently started attending the church, and I chat to her a little bit about how the project is going and what she thought about my sermon on Sunday. As a general rule I don't actually enjoy youth work, nor do I think I'm that good at it, but it really opens doors that I wouldn't otherwise be able to.

Get home around five-ish and have an evening meal with the family, and it's my turn to do bath-time. I speak briefly to a church member, and a vicar from an adjacent parish. The day closes with rugby training. I play for a local team, a reasonably decent standard, and so spend two hours beating people up (good for the soul) and that brings Tuesday to a close. I'm shattered.

James is recently married and has a baby daughter. He and his wife put by time to be together, to pray, to relax. How do you manage your life/work balance?

Ben

I am a Church Army Officer working for the diocese of Manchester as the City Centre Missioner and leader of Sanctus1. The current chapter in the story of the city centre began on 15 June 1996, at peak shopping time when a 3,000 lb IRA bomb exploded in the city centre, injuring more than 200 people and ripping into the fabric of the city's main shopping centre. This event, tragic as it was, was the catalyst for change and over the past eight years the city centre has been rejuvenated as a modern European regional capital. Included within this has been the development of residential apartments, retail, public and cultural spaces such as cathedral gardens and Urbis: the Museum of Urban Life. This has resulted in the residential population rocketing from less than 1,000 in 1996 to currently over 15,000 and according to some estimates an influx of 300,000 people every day. The demographics of the new residential population are fascinating. Over 80% are aged between 16 and 44 and 32% have no faith, twice the city average. City centre apartments are expensive. One recently sold for two million pounds, indicative of the new-found wealth of the city centre.

I was appointed three years ago with a brief to establish a fresh expression of church for the new residents of the city centre. I am part of the staff team at St Ann's church, the city centre parish church, but have close links with Manchester Cathedral and Sacred Trinity, Salford. Over the past three years my ministry has concentrated on establishing Sanctus1, a different sort of church in the city centre of Manchester. We started with a blank sheet of paper and one of the earliest decisions made was that we were ministering to both the residents of the city centre and the city centre users. We were going to operate as a church at the hub of a network, ministering to those who live within the hub and those who are part of the network. Within this context the Anglican parish system is an irrelevance. Sanctus1 meets on Wednesday nights in Sacred Trinity (we have two groups, one at 6.30 and one at 8.00); we also have a monthly Sunday service in either Manchester Cathedral or Sacred Trinity.

The context within which I am ministering, and my ministry in that context, is constantly evolving so this three-day diary will be unique.

Monday

My partner is leaving for work as I begin my breakfast whilst watching the breakfast news. I make myself a coffee before settling down to a time of prayer to start the day.

My day begins in my office where I check my emails. I have not turned my computer on since Friday afternoon and have 34 emails to reply to. The majority are fairly straightforward but there are one or two that require a bit more thought. I am in the process of preparing two services for the Greenbelt festival and there are a number of emails from people concerning this. I check my answer machine; no messages, great! I check the Sanctus1 website. We've been having a few problems with it recently but it all seems to be working now and hits are increasing. There are a few questions on the discussion board which I respond to with further questions.

At 10.30 I have a meeting with my Church Army Northern Operations Manager. We meet every few months and he's about to go on sabbatical so wants to catch up with me beforehand. We have a general chat about the Church Army before moving on to focus on my ministry and the future development plans that I have. I feel quite excited about the possibilities but I am also cautious not to overstretch myself.

I go back to my office and start to prepare for two meetings that I have tomorrow evening concerning the services at Greenbelt. I think the services still need a lot more work and begin to delegate certain tasks to people by email. I get so involved in writing and planning of the services that I fail to notice the time passing. I look at the clock and realise that I only have 50 minutes to prepare and eat my lunch and to catch a bus into the city centre for a meeting at 2.30. I make some lunch, grab my bag and go and wait for the bus. It comes fairly quickly and I arrive at St Ann's for the meeting with the staff team. The meeting is fairly straightforward: we catch up, sharing some concerns that we have, before dealing with a few business items. I choose a couple of dates in the next quarter to preach, and agree to produce some information on Sanctus1 for an exhibition.

After the meeting I have a pastoral appointment with a member of Sanctus1. We meet in a coffee shop in the city centre where he shares a pastoral matter. We talk it through, I agree to pray for him and we discuss how to resolve the situation.

I catch the bus and arrive home at about 5.30; I check my emails and respond to them. I carry on working on administrative tasks until my partner arrives home from work at 6.30. We have a quick chat before both going to do the weekly shop. We get home at about 8.00; she settles down to watch half an hour of TV while I prepare dinner. We eat at 8.30 and then I have a glass of wine whilst relaxing in front of the TV.

Tuesday

Today starts in the same ways as Monday, I respond to my emails and catch up with phone calls, and all seems to be well. I spend the morning continuing to prepare for the meetings I have in the evening. I'm pleased with the two services but need to make sure that the group takes ownership of them.

I catch the bus into town for a meeting over lunch with an artist who is part of Sanctus1 about a piece of work he is producing for us. The meeting is productive and I give him some guidelines and direction regarding the piece. The piece strikes me as rather ambitious; I try to gently discourage him, but he is confident so we proceed.

I spend the afternoon relaxing in the city centre, doing some shopping before going down to Sacred Trinity church. I have a brief chat with another artist who rents a studio space in Sacred Trinity. I spend a couple of hours reading until about 5 p.m. I heat up my dinner in the microwave at Sacred Trinity and then prepare for the meeting I have at 6. People begin to arrive at 5.45 and we have a coffee and begin the meeting at 6; we successfully finalize the first Greenbelt service. At 7.30 the first group leaves and the second group arrives and we finalize the second Greenbelt service.

I lock up the church and leave for home; as I drive home with my partner, I share my feelings about the two meetings: I was pleased with them both but felt that I really had to keep the two groups focused on the service as they were easily sidetracked. There was some conflict within the first meeting that I resolved, but I am aware that I need to tackle the issue directly. I talk this through with my partner and she suggests some strategies for dealing with this.

I get home at 9.15 and spend some time relaxing, before having a bath and going to bed.

Wednesday

I have a slow start to Wednesday. I get up late as I know I will be working late, and start work at about 11 a.m. I reply to my emails and contact the person who is leading Sanctus1 tonight; everything is ready for the evening. I prepare and eat my lunch before going back to my office to prepare a sermon for Sunday as I'm preaching at St Ann's.

At about 4.30 I catch the bus into the city centre and make my way down to Sacred Trinity. I prepare Sacred Trinity for the evening meeting. Tonight's Sanctus1 is slightly different from usual; we are sharing a meal together before embarking on an Architecture and Spirituality walk of the City Centre.

People arrive at 6.30; everyone brings a dish and we eat together. There are about 30 people. I spend some time chatting with a few of the newer people to make sure that they are feeling welcomed. We wash up and then at 8:00 some other people arrive and we begin the walk. We travel round in seven groups. I leave in the final one and follow the Architecture and Spirituality guide. It is fascinating to compare the different spiritual spaces in the city centre. We all reconvene at a pub in the city centre before making our way back to Sacred Trinity and then home. I arrive home at 11.15. Tired out, I go to bed.

Ben talks of exploring a 'fresh expression of church'. What do you consider to be the strengths and weaknesses of his description of Sanctus 1 as a church that relies more upon networks of people than a parish or geographical area, and that offers worship which is not on a Sunday in order to reach the workers and residents of city centre Manchester?

(For further reading, see *Mission-Shaped Church*, Church House Publishing, 2004.)

1

LEARNING TO READ THE SIGNS OF THE TIMES: MINISTRY IN A CHANGING WORLD

In the previous section six ministers gave accounts of their lives and ministries, six stories that reveal much about church ministry in today's society, and how they make connections and build community in the local context. In this chapter we examine what they wrote in the light of current thinking about society, and think further about the sort of ministry that churches need to offer. Lifelong learning and supervision in ministry requires some thought about the shape of contemporary church life, and that in turn begs questions of the nature of the world with which ministry engages.

The Global and Local

> Globalization in all its aspects – the collapse of the bipolar world and of socialism as an economic alternative, the dominance of neoliberal capitalism, the advances in communications technologies, and the migration of peoples – all are making the world a different place. (Schreiter, 2002, p. 85)

If the world is changing under the pressure of some or all of the factors that Schreiter names above, then there are indications that the shape of the church is evolving too. Ben's work in the middle of urban Manchester illustrates how he experiments with the way in which church meets the challenges of an increasingly globalized world, helping people to reflect upon the pressures and pleasures of urban life. Although many indicators suggest that traditional churchgoing is declining (see Brierley 2000), there are signs of growth and development in new directions, towards a mixed mode of traditional patterns of worship with innovative styles of engagement with local society. The six ministers present a set of cameos of ministry in today's world and indicate how they engage in varying ways with some of the dynamics of a globalized world. To analyse further what they wrote, I draw on writers who offer social analysis that addresses different issues that arise in the six accounts.

In his book *The New Catholicity*, Schreiter shows that in a post-cold-war world, neo-liberal capitalism has become monolithic. No longer is there bipolarity between capitalism and socialism. The world now is multipolar, with many conflicting political agendas and different alliances within a capitalism that spreads throughout the world. Communication grows ever more sophisticated, and creates a global network, where information and resources, both financial and human, circulate as the market requires.

Schreiter describes the fall-out of the global market as well. One of the characteristics of global capitalism is its ability to move capital quickly, focusing upon short-term profit rather than long-term investment in people or place. Some people, roughly twenty per cent, are enriched fabulously, but many more are not only not better off, but are driven deeper into poverty and misery (2002, p. 7). Along with finance, people also are forced to circulate around the world, fleeing homelands destroyed through violence or extreme poverty. There is a growing polarization between those who 'have' and those who do not benefit from the promise of post-industrial global capitalism.

Manuel Castells, in *The Information Age*, says much the same thing. He characterizes the world in which we live as one shaped primarily by information. The information age has superseded the industrial capitalism and national state that transformed cultures, created wealth and induced poverty during the twentieth century (vol. 2, pp. 1–2). With a revolution in information technology, a new form of society comes into existence – the network society – which 'transforms all domains of social and economic life' (vol. 3, p. 368). This network society needs to be understood as 'based on a space of flows' (vol. 3, p. 367), where 'networks of capital, labor, information, and markets link up, through technology, valuable functions, people and localities around the world' (vol. 3, p. 368).

Again, the downside. Castells describes 'territories deprived of value and interest for the dynamics of global capitalism', with resultant 'social exclusion and irrelevance of segments of societies, of areas of cities, of regions, and of entire countries' (vol. 3, p. 368). He calls such areas and regions the 'Fourth World'. In such a world a growing number of people become irrelevant to the dynamics of the new global capitalism. They do not have the resources or educational opportunities to stay afloat, let alone surf the Internet society, which requires the ability to network, to work flexitime, to respond by reprogramming oneself within the endlessly changing market (vol. 3, p. 372).

Another consequence for work, according to Castells, is what he calls 'generic labor', where people are ultimately interchangeable with machines. 'What is happening', he comments, 'is that the mass of generic labor circulates in a variety of jobs, increasingly occasional jobs, with a great deal of discontinuity' (vol. 3, p. 375). The resulting fragmentation leads ultimately to a loss of a stable relationship to employment, weak bargaining power, and higher levels of major crises in the lives of individuals and their families. The polarization of 'have' and 'have not' becomes consolidated in areas such as Liz, Geoff and James minister in, where extreme poverty creates 'black holes of informational capitalism' (vol. 3, p. 376), as Castells calls the terrible plight and the cost borne by the victims of the new global trends.

'The Double Whammy'

John Atherton writes from many years' experience of and reflection upon the interface between church and society in Britain today. His 2003 book *Marginalization* charts current trends of decline, certainly in urban contexts like Manchester, decline that he suggests might be terminal by 2040 (p. 31). His concern is that 'churches facing most difficulties were disproportionately located in those urban communities facing most difficulties' (p. 2), a phenomenon he calls 'a double whammy'. But such churches are merely indicative of a wider crisis facing the churches of today, a crisis that is multilayered and multifaceted (p. 58), involving complex registers of exclusion, marginalization and deprivation in the face of changing national and global contexts. The double whammy of double whammies, he says, is 'that combination of increasing marginalization of peoples, nations and environments, and increasing marginalization of our understandings of God and church from that marginalized context'. Churches that continue to survive (even if only just) in such communities provide the opportunity for Christianity to continue to engage.

For Atherton, economic analysis and political engagement are essential ingredients to working towards a better world. *Marginalization* explores ways in which different economic solutions are being developed that counter the power of global capitalism and enable wealth and resources to be used more equitably. He also argues that there are issues of power that require addressing: marginalized groups in today's society find it difficult to engage in political and decision-making processes. To analyse this further, he turns to the work of Iris Marion Young. In *Inclusion and Democracy*, she argues that democratic structures need to be much more inclusive so that different perspectives can be heard in political forums where usually they are not. She advocates a form of inclusive democracy that takes into account the ways in which people can be excluded from political structures because of their gender, 'race', poverty and class – factors which can coalesce into a matrix of oppression (2000, pp. 92–3). Democratic processes benefit greatly if they can incorporate different perspectives, and political bodies need to find ways of including different voices and showing solidarity with people and local groups who are usually marginalized. Young calls this 'differentiated solidarity'. She writes:

> I offer an alternative ideal of social and political inclusion that I call 'differentiated solidarity'. This idea shares with an ideal of integration a commitment to combat exclusion and foster individual freedom . . . [It] affirms that groups nevertheless dwell together, whether they like it or not, within a set of problems and relationships of structural interdependence that bring with them obligations of justice. (2000, p. 197)

Lynn illustrated a form of differentiated solidarity in her sensitivity to the couple who wanted to be married, and her awareness of the different way in which they expressed themselves and the 'frail bridge' they crossed in order to come to her with their request. Her observation that the café staff were 'too polite' alerted her to the need for a different way of hearing in order to engage with how and what they were saying. Young would affirm the inclusive way in which Lynn achieved this as she and the couple moved towards a decision together. Lynn was happy for meetings and administrative tasks to be interrupted: another example of a flexible and inclusive approach that enabled those usually excluded to feel supported and valued as contributors to the projects at Millhill.

Geoff and the local community network thought that 'there is a massive gap between local authority processes and the way in which people relate to what is going on in their community'. Their work to involve the community in reshaping the services which would follow the end of the local partnership body and the Single Regeneration Budget is an illustration of how churches can start to insist on greater inclusivity in local democratic processes. James's work at the local youth project – 'just eating biscuits, chatting to the kids who are involved in petty crime and drugs' – was a beginning towards a greater trust on the basis of listening to their discourse, not insisting that they speak his language.

Atherton writes of marginalized churches that there is a need to empower voiceless people and communities to respond to changing global and local dynamics. He argues that churches have to gain a deeper sense of their own identity and distinctive contribution to society, so that their effectiveness is based upon 'being clearer about our identity as worship, nurture and mission'. The ability to engage in the local community and make partnerships to build more effective communities (2003, p. 130) entails being a church which includes 'dialogue and outreach through worship and service as its distinctive heart' (p. 132). Those who minister within churches need to be effective at functioning in plural settings with an analysis of power and dominance, a theme we return to at the end of Chapter 6. The six living human documents all indicate some involvement in these processes towards greater inclusivity and the necessity of hearing different voices within democratic and decision-making processes.

Each of the ministers can be seen to be resisting the impact of the processes of globalization upon their localities. Schreiter points out that 'there is no "local" any more that is not touched by powerful outside forces' (2002, p. ix). Castells believes that political power is likely to be most effective in local networks, communities of resistance and identity-based social movements (vol. 3, p. 383). He writes:

The era of globalization of the economy is also the era of localization of polity. What local and regional governments lack in power and resources, they make up in flexibility and networking. They are the only match, if any, to the dynamism of global networks of wealth and information. (vol. 3, p. 388)

Jean's ministry, in a rural setting, illustrates well the same sort of networking that James, Lynn and Geoff engaged in. She meets with housing enablers, with the South-West Rural Affairs Forum, with the NFU, with the local Agenda 21 activists, with the Farm Crisis Network, as well as negotiating with the Health Authority, and considers whether to be on the picket line at 4 a.m. Her flexible approach relies for its effectiveness on good communication with different organizations and groups at the local and regional levels.

Churches: Engagement and Resistance

Schreiter talks of the resistance offered as part of what the churches can do (2002, p. 73), and the six accounts of ministers working in local contexts show them addressing issues raised by migrations and asylum seeking, crime, and the polarization of wealth and poverty. James, in a church that is 'hugely' involved in work with asylum seekers, mentions how he collaborates with other churches in the area. He develops all sorts of links with the wider community, particularly with young people and local housing officers, in an effort to counter the crime in his estate. We heard how he tried to help an asylum seeker find a lawyer. Lynn, working with Jean the project worker, shows how a new form of church could become not just a haven for those who struggle with poverty and exclusion, but also potentially a place of local political engagement, bringing together social workers and health visitors for concerted action that was relevant to the locality. Her involvement and imagination has transformed a failing, nearly moribund church into an agency which addresses the issues that face the local community: poverty, drug abuse and early death, and consequent childhood bereavement for those who lose parents. Jean's way of working takes her out and about, networking and negotiating with all sorts of people on a wide range of concerns that are the local pressure points of global issues.

All six ministers show the real complexity of working for the church in today's world. They each show an engagement with the issues that affect the communities and individuals around them, as well as providing leadership in the worship of their congregations and churches. In each of the stories different aspects of the world emerge as local challenge, indications of 'a world troubled by its own promise', as Castells describes it (vol. 3, p. 390). Leonie Sandercock in her book *Cosmopolis II: Mongrel Cities* (2003) stresses the importance of stories of community resistance 'from people whose life space is at stake in the urban and regional development processes' (p. 56). She writes from the perspective of a city planner, and offers inspiring examples of how local mobilization can make a difference in localities that have been forgotten by the world of the rich. Groups and individuals who seek to make a difference to those who are disadvantaged by the dynamics of global capitalism can, with good analysis and shrewd engagement, become powerful practitioners in local and regional politics.

Those who offer ministry in today's world need to understand these dynamics and be able to respond by drawing on the resources of tradition and scripture, and finding ways of being church in imaginative ways appropriate to the situations they face. The lifelong learning of those who offer public ministry needs to equip them to live in communities of faith, imaginatively and flexibly, reactive and proactive, taking the living traditions of faith and reinterpreting them in new circumstances.

Sandercock's book emphasizes the importance of created space – buildings, public areas, streets. Lynn's experience of creating what has been called a 'temple' space in the locality would support Sandercock's thesis. Her presence and imagination has led to a revival – but not following previous patterns of church. In his study (in Cameron *et al.*, 2005), Storrar comments of Lynn's work at Millhill: 'Church membership remains small but the church building has been transformed into an open, welcoming place where local people belong and find hope for their lives and community.' He interviewed Lynn and Jean. Lynn commented that they have given up trying to meet the denomination's expectations of a parish church or ministry, with its organizations, congregational visiting and constant hunt for office-bearers. Storrar says that

> Lynn typically spends her day in the church building in a ministry of presence and encounter with the café clientele or mourners in the sanctuary. Church members more willingly serve in these new forms of ministry than on committees. All are in the process of becoming something, or rather, some-place different. New people and resources are involved: through the active participation of the local community and through partnership with external funding bodies. In one of the poorest communities in Britain, the Gospel is inhabited and walked, rather than measured. (2005, p. 177)

This is a good example of what 'performative' ministry looks like: the gospel comes alive in the practices of the church as it serves and inspires the community around. Lynn commented to Storrar in an interview about the changing purpose of the building:

> There is a theory about doing things off the premises and starting up say a shop or something in the community, particularly in communities like this. People have gone into the idea of house churches and moving away from buildings. I think if you scrape the surface of most of the people in the church, they still feel that it should be around the church . . . and I feel it should be in the church. Not because I want the gathering in here but because I think it is important to make that connection, to be honest about it and say, 'this is who we are', and that the project will be run by people who . . . it doesn't matter if they have faith or not . . . we need them to do this job for the children . . . but there is something about linking it in to the memorial chapel and the tree and

the services of remembrance we have had there for children as well as adults. (2005, p. 194)

Lynn's ministry at Millhill shows an imaginative, flexible approach to the needs of the local community and the transformation of a dilapidated church building to form an inclusive, useful resource to people, generating income and employment. This is a ministry of resistance to the global trends that create the black holes of deprivation that Castells describes. Lynn works with others on projects based on a good analysis of local need.

In the six living human documents there is a sense of 'it doesn't have to be like this!' A sense of prophecy and hope in the face of the despair of multiple deprivation permeates their accounts. As Schreiter says, 'local situations are not powerless . . . They work out all kinds of arrangements' (2002, p. 12) to resist the processes of globalization that fragment and can decimate local communities.

For our six ministers the worship and prayer that the church offers provides the sustenance and hope to continue, both for them and for the communities in which they work. For Lynn the church building was important as a place to connect the Christian faith with the needs of the community. The church café, memorial chapel and counselling centre functioned like the outer and inner courtyards of a temple, leading local people through different zones into the ritual place of worship at the heart. Nor was the worship escapist in the life and suffering of this community. As Lynn put it:

It seems to me that the importance of worship is where life is and so that's when you come back to the café, and you come back to the suffering and you come back to, how do you bring this back into the life and worship of the church? (2005, p. 178)

The six ministers all work with others within their own teams and churches, ecumenically and with agencies, other networks and other organizations, from Government-based ones, to campaigning groups and charities, to schools and projects like Millhill Hope for bereaved children. They minister not so much as individuals, but as part of larger groups. For Castells, identity is not an individual attribute but is formed collectively. He argues that identity emerges and becomes a collective agency of social transformation, constructed around projects which go on the offensive to create a better way of life with the long term in view (vol. 2, p. 67). Graham emphasizes something similar when she writes that ministry 'is always necessarily corporate and social, in that personal belief and commitment is preceded by our inhabitation of a multiplicity of faith-communities (some of them religious) in which the telling and retelling of narrative and meaning is already taking place' (1996, p. 39). For her, the agent of Christian practice is the community of faith which forms individuals and actions of justice and hope through a wide range of sacramental, moral, therapeutic practices that create new knowledge and disclose new theological insights. She explains how practices that continue to reinterpret the living texts of tradition shape ministry and agency in creative, subversive, inspirational and prophetic ways (1996, p. 108). The six stories show how ministry is always embedded in particular contexts and communities.

But it is important, I think, to stress the individual agency of ministry alongside the corporate engagement: each of the ministers is a crucial agent in the locality, playing a representative role, and able to initiate and consolidate ideas and visions, leading others towards new possibilities. As Sandercock points out, the role of individual agent is often central to a project as someone who is good at 'organizing hope, negotiating fears, mediating collective memories of identity and belonging, and daring to take risks' (2003, p. 179). The minister must often inspire others and motivate, taking risks when necessary, ready to fail and be disappointed when things don't work. The experience recorded in the stories above illustrates how important it is for a minister to be able to listen to criticism with openness and the ability to adapt and change.

The six ministers work in very different circumstances and illustrate something of the way a contemporary church minister is involved in wide range of engagement in political issues at a local, regional and national level. They show how ministers need to be both reactive and proactive. To do this effectively they must analyse the economic and political situation, and engage with political bodies that make a difference to the places and people with whom they work. The minister will find her or himself representing the needs of others, speaking as an advocate on a wide range of issues, enabling others to assume greater responsibility in their lives. They need to be flexible and able to 'multi-task' work and family commitments. The ministries we have looked at here are 'performative' in the sense Graham uses the word: the ministries perform and construct faith as the values of justice and inclusion are embodied and realized in practices that attempt to transform the lives of people in their areas of work, life and ministry.

Three days in *your* life . . .

Keep a journal account of your life and ministry over three days.

When you have done so, read back what you have written. How would you respond to the question:

In what ways is your ministry 'performative'?

A World Troubled by Its Own Promise

One of the promises that troubles the world (surprisingly, not mentioned except fleetingly by James – and then more as a 'trouble' than a 'promise') is cultural diversity as people migrate, seeking safety and well being, asylum from violence, a better future. An obvious consequence of global capitalism is an increased mixing of society in terms of culture and ethnicity, although as Alibhai-Brown (2001) and others argue, British national identity has never been 'pure', has always been an evolving hybrid (see Fryer, 1984). Sandercock (2003) writes of cities around the world where life is increasingly multicultural and where she is led to think about identity and belonging, home and nation, freedom and fear (p. xiii). The promise of the world, as she sees it, is found as people seek to live together in a 'new urban condition in which difference, otherness, fragmentation, splintering, multiplicity, heterogeneity, diversity, plurality prevail' (p. 1). The promise is there of 'the possibility of living alongside others who are different, learning from them, creating new worlds with them, instead of fearing them' (p. 1). From her extensive experience of working and advising town planners and politicians in many cities and neighbourhoods from Sydney to Vancouver, from Birmingham to Chicago, from Frankfurt to Cape Town, she writes of her dreams of Cosmopolis, in the recognition that hope and utopia are essential to build a better world.

Her work is wide-ranging. Planners who build the Cosmopolis, she suggests, need to have five qualities. They need to be critical, creative, therapeutic, political, and audacious (p. 8). This seems like a good list to appropriate for church ministers who work in the twenty-first century, where many of the global issues created by the flows of people will call for a gospel of justice, love and hope in a multicultural world. The creation of inclusive societies does and will present a challenge to those for whom religion operates in exclusive ways, as a fundamentalist ideology based upon a concept of cultural or religious purity. Sandercock argues for the need for public persons to be able to analyse the situation and negotiate inclusively in multicultural contexts, respectful of differences of culture and able to work with conflict.

Are Sandercock's five qualities required for dealing with the mongrel cities of the twenty-first century useful to you as you consider your engagement with a world troubled by its own promise?

In what ways are you:

- Critical
- Creative
- Therapeutic
- Political
- Audacious?

The ground we have covered in this chapter presents a not unhopeful analysis. Graham and Castells put a great deal of emphasis upon the transformative power of projects and identities that are able to respond and resist the negative, destructive forces that can wreak so much damage in local communities. The key to action is the ability to access information and use it to serve the creation of a better world, and we saw above how the ministers put communication high on their agenda, whether in face-to-face meetings with other colleagues, or out in the community as networking and gossip, or via the Internet and email. The minister as networker, as someone who is able to help others to find a voice and act to make a more just world, becomes a predominant image. This is ministry that reveals a sense of identity that is able to reflect upon itself and be critical of its own effectiveness in order to be proactive and reactive in local and global contexts. Instead of a ministry formed to provide the same traditions of worship and service, ministry becomes transformative and performative in any number of different contexts made complex by global and local dynamics. Lifelong learning, as a reflexive and reflective practice, is what can sustain and develop such a sense of identity.

2

WHAT KIND OF LEARNING? DEVELOPMENTS WITHIN THEOLOGICAL EDUCATION

If you start to read here, you will approach supervision from the perspective of theological education. I chart some relevant developments in educational theory and, by using the Church of England as a case study, I show how those developments have been absorbed within theological education. In the documents surveyed in this chapter, supervision is increasingly recognized as an important component.

Education: Commodity or Process?

In the Introduction, I noted a shift from a didactic teaching approach to an appreciation of 'the learning adult'. That shift can be traced to the work of educationalists like Polanyi who wrote in 1969 of the need for education to be seen not as the acquisition of knowledge as a *commodity*, but rather as a *process* of change and growth. In the 1970s, Paulo Freire's hugely influential book *Pedagogy of the Oppressed* stressed the importance of moving away from a 'banking' approach to education, where knowledge is seen as something banked up in the recipient, to an understanding of knowledge as something that changes and develops in use and action. Written in the context of Latin America, Freire's work has remained an influential text that reminds theologians and educators of the transformative power of education, especially for those who are oppressed and powerless.

Jennifer Moon (2004) presents two views of learning (and you can see the continuity with Freire): the 'building bricks' view and the 'network' view. She writes:

> In the first model of learning, the assumption is maintained that material of teaching is somehow 'taken in' or 'absorbed' by the learner, and retained in the same form as it is encountered (bar some modification because of memory) . . . The learner would then, at a later stage, be able to represent it reasonably closely to the form in which it was presented by the teacher. This accords with the 'building a brick wall' view of learning in which the teacher provides for the learner the 'bricks of knowledge'. It is assumed that the teacher knows how these will fit the pattern of the wall. The wall – knowledge – is thus built up. (p. 16)

Moon contrasts this rather static image of knowledge and education with a more dynamic, 'constructivist' view where learning and knowledge are more like a 'vast and flexible network of ideas and feelings' and where new ideas are linked into the network and assimilated into the existing map of someone's understanding of the world. She says:

> the process of learning is not, therefore, about the accumulation of material of learning, but about the process of changing conceptions. Given that learning usually implies that a person becomes progressively wiser and better at learning and understanding, a better phrase might be 'transforming conceptions'. (p. 17)

Moon suggests that learning is a dynamic process in which someone continually constructs and reconstructs a view of the world as she or he makes sense of what is experienced. The network of interlinked ideas and understanding changes as new experience and learning is incorporated in a process that transforms the person's outlook. The advantage of such a view of knowledge is its dynamic nature. Rather than the static accumulation of bricks that build a wall, a network suggests a map of interlinking pathways and connections that stretch out in various directions. Some directions will be relevant at any given time and will be where the current learning occurs; others are byways and avenues waiting for future exploration.

Education: Experience and Reflection

If adult education is much more about the development of a network or map of knowledge, the way in which experience is viewed and integrated with the existing body of knowledge becomes important. D. A. Kolb developed a scheme for understanding the way in which experience can be seen to contribute to the learning process, and his cycle of action and reflection has been widely used and adapted. He suggested that to learn from experience begins with the experience itself, which can be observed and reflected upon. Those observations and reflections become the basis of a working theory, from which appropriate action is discerned. Action in experience then becomes a new experience which is then subjected to further reflection, in a process of continual action and reflection (see Kolb, 1984). This idea of a cyclical pattern of reflection upon experience has influenced many and is represented in various learning cycles and spirals within the discipline of practical theology and theological reflection (for example, Green, 2000; Ballard and Pritchard, 1996). Foskett and Lyall use Kolb's cycle as the basis for their chapter 'Learning and Experience' (1990, p. 14). They trace the experience of a curate as he explores with his supervisor a visit to Mrs Brown. Beginning with the experience of that visit, Foskett and Lyall show how he is led on to reflect and observe about what happened, and then to the third stage of making meaning and understanding, through practice in the future (pp. 14–15).

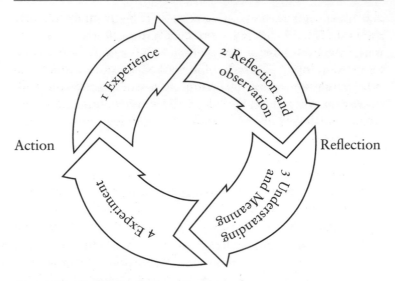

Figure 3: Kolb's Learning Cycle.

Moon acknowledges the debt to Kolb in her work on how experience is to be used in education (2004, p. 114). Moon herself thinks that the encounter with an experience that offers learning will involve the following bulleted points (see p. 115):

- Recognition of a need to resolve something
- Clarification of the issue
- Reviewing and recollecting
- Reviewing feelings/the emotional state
- Processing of knowledge and ideas
- Eventual resolution, possible transformation and action
- Possible action

The next time you face a situation that you think lends itself to using these seven bullet points, use your learning journal to write up how you work through each of them.

And then, afterwards, consider the question: In what ways has this exercise enabled you to learn from experience?

If Kolb and others have focused on learning from *experience*, then others have thought more deeply about the processes of reflection that occur as people learn. Donald Schön (1983, 1987) developed the idea of reflection in professional and other situations where structures of learning were not well-defined or were unpredictable. For him the gaining of know-ledge-in-action is dynamic and goes beyond having to 'think about it'.

> When we have learned how to do something, we can execute smooth sequences of activity, recognition, decision, and adjustment without having, as we say, to 'think about it'. Our spontaneous knowing-in-action usually gets us through the day. On occasion, however, it doesn't. A familiar routine produces an unexpected result . . . although the usual actions produce the usual outcomes, we find something odd about them because, for some reason, we have begun to look at them in a new way. All such experiences, pleasant and unpleasant, contain an element of *surprise* . . . In an attempt to preserve the constancy of our usual patterns of knowing-in-action, we may respond to surprise by brushing it aside . . . or we may respond to it by reflection. (1987, p. 26, his emphasis)

He goes on to say that reflection happens in one of two ways: either we think back over the action; or we reflect in the midst of action where 'our thinking serves to reshape what we are doing while we are doing it'. Schön's work has been very influential across a wide range of professional disciplines as professional educators have seen the value of enabling prac-titioners to reflect upon and learn from their experience (see Flyvbjerg, 2001; Bolton, 2003).

Since 1990, Moon comments, the theory and practice of reflection have attained a much more significant role in educational contexts (2004, p. 82). She offers further think-ing on the nature of reflection, differentiating between *surface* and *deep* reflection. The former will tend to be descriptive and more dependent upon the 'banking' or brick wall approach to learning, where a learner will try to absorb as much content as is necessary for the task at hand: a 'cramming' method. Surface reflection is likely to be short-term and rather unsatisfactory and will often engender levels of anxiety that can prove counter-productive to the end goal of the learning. Someone who is engaged upon 'deeper' reflection will 'seek the underpinning principles and endeavour to relate the material to previous knowledge and understanding' (p. 59). They will be well motivated and interested in what they learn, and show a sense of satisfaction, particularly when 'the penny drops' and they gain new insights that transform their former cognitive map.

You can see how Ben reflects upon the evening as he drives home with his partner on Tuesday evening. 'I share my feelings about the two meetings: I was pleased with them both but felt that I really had to keep the two groups focused on the service as they were easily sidetracked. There was some conflict within the first meeting that I resolved, but I am aware that I need to tackle the issue directly. I talk this through with my partner and she suggests some strategies for dealing with this.'

Schön talked of reflection after the event, looking back, as Ben is doing here. He also talked of reflection in the midst of action.

Can you identify examples of each from your own experience?

A time when you have looked back in order to think about how you could do something differently?

Another time when you have reflected as you have been doing something?

Write both examples in your learning journal.

Learning can be better understood, then, by using the 'network' image, with experience providing a crucial element, and the need to develop skills in 'deep' reflection. This underpins how lifelong learning is understood, and supervision can provide tools and resources to support ministers who wish to continue to develop skills in reflective practice as a key component in lifelong learning.

I have used the Anglican Church as a case study, but during this time all of the main churches, and particularly the United Reformed Church[2] and the Methodist Church,[3] have recognized the need to work more closely with each other, both in the development of policy and in the delivery of courses and training (for further details for the Church of Scotland[4] and the Baptist Union,[5] see footnotes below).

---

[2] For the United Reformed Church, see *CME Learning for Life*, June 2001; *Making CME work*, May 2003. Further information from the Training Office, The United Reformed Church, 86 Tavistock Place, London, WC1H 9RT; email training@urc.org.uk; webpage: www.urc.org.uk

[3] For the Methodist Church, see *The Making of Ministry: the Report of the Ministerial Training Policy Working Group to the Methodist Council*, September 1996; *Handbook for Probation: Formation in Ministry*, September 2003; and other Formation in Ministry discussion papers available from Methodist Church House, 25 Marylebone Road, London NW1 5JR; email formationinministry@methodistchurch.org.uk

[4] For the Church of Scotland, see the Board of Ministry report to the General Assembly, May 2000.

[5] For the Baptist Union, go to www.baptist.org.uk

A Case Study: Developments in Theological Education in the Church of England

The ball started to roll with the publication in 1987 of the church report *Education for the Church's Ministry*, popularly known as ACCM 22. (ACCM stands for Advisory Council for the Church's Ministry. All the Anglican reports referred to here are available from www.chpublishing.co.uk.) This established a clear theological basis for education which took seriously the engagement of the church in the world. Paragraph 27 has been seen as fundamental:

> 27. The Church's task is to *serve the mission of God in the world*. So, regardless of the diversity of situations within which it does so, its task is fundamentally twofold: to proclaim the creative activity of God by which the world is constituted in its proper nature by God, affirming the world so far as it reflects its proper nature; and to proclaim the redemptive activity of God by which the world is once again given its proper being, thereby to be fulfilled according to God's purposes. In this task it follows, and by its nature seeks to conform to, the work of God – through Jesus Christ and by the Holy Spirit – in and for the world, in order to bring the world to its proper relation to God. The task of proclaiming God's word of creation and redemption is one, not simply of interpreting the world and its future according to the promises of God, but of realizing their consequences by conforming Church and world to the purposes of God.

This passage is fundamental because it signals the need for a good theological underpinning for educational programmes. It also sets the ministry of the church within the wide picture of God's relationship with the world. The report then addressed the diversity of people offering for ministry in the Church of England, and argued that theological colleges and courses should provide the means whereby men and women could receive the necessary formation, or at least the necessary foundation for a lifelong process (p. 9). It called for an end to the core curriculum set and assessed centrally, with the proposal that college and course staffs devise their own educational packages to be validated and assessed centrally every five years.

It argued for greater attention to the ways in which adults learn, and a move away from too much emphasis upon the presentation and assimilation of information by lectures towards more opportunities for critical discussion and theological engagement with experience (p. 20). This move reflects the work of Polyani (1969) and Freire (1970) who, as we have seen, argued that knowledge should not be seen as a commodity, but as a process. The writers of the report found the educational programmes in colleges and courses were fragmented, with little direction provided by staff and little ownership by students in either establishing priorities or evaluating what had been achieved (p. 21). Again, such emphases are to the fore in education across the spectrum today, and are essential if learning is to be 'deep' and transformative.

ACCM 22 offered three questions for consideration by the wider church in order to set the context in which colleges and courses could then develop educational programmes. Those three questions were:

- What ordained ministry does the Church of England require?
- What is the shape of the educational programme best suited for equipping people to exercise this ministry?
- What are the appropriate means of assessing suitability for ordination to exercise this ministry?

The aim, as that report saw it, of theological education was to enable the church to manifest its own nature in its ministry and to fulfil its task of 'serving the mission of God in the world' (p. 27). This mission was carried forward by the whole people of God, within whom the ordained ministry had a particular task of 'recognizing, coordinating and distributing the ministry of others' (p. 29).

The educational programmes and methods required to equip such ministry were seen as a lifelong process of personal development, with the fundamental aim of enabling 'the student to grow in those personal qualities by which, with and through the corporate ministry of the Church, the creative and redemptive activity of God may be proclaimed and realised in the world' (p. 37). To do this, the courses and colleges 'must provide a deep and intelligent inquiry into the Christian Scripture and tradition . . . while also relating that to present circumstances' (p. 40).

So this report challenged the Church of England on two main counts. First, it presented ministry as the church's task in carrying forward the mission of God in the world, challenging the church as a whole to address the question of what sort of ministry was required. Secondly, it recommended greater thought to the content and methods of theological education as a foundation of lifelong formation. Theological education, it recommended, needed to be rigorous in terms of scripture and tradition, but needed also to develop in the ordinand skills of social analysis and reflection.

ACCM 22 set the agenda for the Church of England in theological education. A number of reports followed that developed different aspects implicit within ACCM 22.[6] In what follows I briefly review these documents, charting the

---

[6] The staffs of the colleges and courses responded with ABM (Advisory Board of Ministry) paper no. 1 in 1990, and work was done in 1992 on integration and assessment (ABM 3). In 1992 *A Way Ahead* was produced which was a report to the House of Bishops on Theological Colleges and Courses. In 1998 a report was made on Local Non-Stipendiary Ministry, entitled *Stranger in the Wings*. In the same year *Beginning Public Ministry* offered guidelines for ministerial formation and personal development for the first four years after ordination. In 2001 *Mind The Gap* reported on continuing ministerial education and in 2003 two further important documents were published: one reviewing ACCM 22, entitled *Mission and Ministry: The Church's validation framework for theological education*, and another that year which offered a radical proposal for the structure and funding for *Formation for Ministry within a Learning Church*, otherwise known as the 'Hind Report'.

shift in theological emphasis towards a Trinitarian underpinning, and the increasing value given to reflective practice and supervision, as the educational basis shifts from a traditional 'banking' method, to use Freire's expression, to more of an appreciation of education as a learning *process*.

When the staffs of the colleges and courses responded in 1990 to ACCM 22, they shifted the theological emphasis in a more Trinitarian direction. Instead of the frame of 'the creative and redemptive action of God in the world', and the church conforming to God's mission, this document proposed that the Trinity become the framework, enabling *relationship* to be central to the ministry of the church. The Trinity offered a way of understanding power relations that are not hierarchical or authoritarian, but participatory, not only in institutions, but also in God's mission in the world. Their response provided a basis for an understanding of theological method: of how theology can be done, given the fact of the diversity of Christian belief and religious pluralism. The ability to be both theologically critical and affirmative about diversity, without evading tension or conflict, could, they suggested, develop from Trinitarian doctrine, and thereby provide the basis for understanding the church's engagement in the world (p. 23).

The staff response affirmed the interactive nature of theology with culture. The doctrine of the Trinity underpins further reflection on the need for ministers to be able to live creatively with diversity in the world. The report noted two pitfalls that are often seen when different perspectives are encountered: either there is an over-emphasis on a loose and pragmatic kind of unity based upon benign tolerance and coexistence; or unity is based, on the other hand, upon conformity (p. 37). The report advocates the need for the ordained minister to develop the patience to stay with uncertainty, complexity and conflict, rather than reaching after premature resolution. They write that these considerations underline the dimension of mystery always involved in speaking of and relating to God as Trinity. The mystery of God is seen in the multiplicity and rich variety of participation in God and of speech about God, as distinct from either a uniform encounter with God or the impossibility of speech about God at all. In the following chapter I develop this emphasis upon the Trinity, and this need for ministers to be able to live with the tensions of ministry in a complex and diverse world.

The authors of the report had much to say about the *identity* of the minister:

> Emphasis now falls on a conception of *identity in relation* of the ordained. This is not, we believe, a sign of the mere abandonment of a concern with the 'being' (rather than just the pragmatic function) of the ordained person: quite the contrary. It is to locate the being of the minister within the dual and dynamic context of the active being of God, and the life of the whole believing community. (p. 40)

This comment recalls us to the central question of how the lifelong learning of a minister can be carried forward so that their identity-in-relation is seen as self-aware; able to relate in diverse contexts with diverse groups and individuals and minister creatively in a changing world.

ACCM 22 argued that theological education should extend beyond the initial period of training and be seen as a lifelong process. This was developed in 1998 with *Beginning Public Ministry* which produced guidelines for supervisors, parishes and curates during the four years immediately after ordination. It indicates what can properly be expected of a supervisor and training parish, and offers a list of expectations that the newly ordained minister might realize by the end of the four years. It offers a detailed check-list of all the areas to be considered in drawing up an individual training programme. The report argued that such documentation needed to be sensitive to local contexts and drawn up in the light of initial formal training through college or course, setting the educational opportunities in the context of continuous professional development and lifelong learning.

The traditional relationship of master/apprentice between

supervisor (or training incumbent as this role tends to be called in the Church of England) and curate gives way, in times of increasing collaborative ministry, to the understanding of a supervisor who fulfils the role of coach or learning facilitator, there to develop the foundation laid by the initial training period. The role now involved oversight of the ordinand's spirituality, academic base, self-understanding and understanding of the pastoral context, and was to enable a wide-range of ministerial skills and techniques to be acquired. The report required regular supervision sessions and ongoing assessment of learning throughout the curacy.

If you are a supervisor with responsibility for the learning of another in a pastoral setting, how do you assess yourself against this list in the report *Beginning Public Ministry* (1998, pp. 8–9)? Are you:

An experienced minister who:

- is settled in the parish or pastorate and will make a commitment to stay for the majority of duration of the training period;
- is already engaged in in-service training and is willing to undertake further training associated with becoming a training minister, e.g. a course in the skills of supervision, and consultation days;
- is possessed of a mature degree of self-awareness and understanding of his/her own:
  - o strengths and weaknesses in ministry;
  - o psychological make-up and personality;
- has ability to make appropriate relationships with a colleague in training;
- has a genuine desire to be a training minister as distinct from merely wanting an assistant;
- is prepared to take into consideration a curate or student minister's experience in terms of previous employment and responsibilities;
- has an ability to help the curate or student minister in

the process of integrating his/her theological studies with ministerial experience;

- has an understanding of learning styles and cycles in adult learning;
- is willing to make a distinction between staff meetings and supervision sessions and to organise both on a regular basis;
- has a personal theological and spiritual stance which is creative and flexible and is thereby:
  - able to articulate his/her own theological position;
  - ready to work with a student minister or curate of a different theological position and spiritual disposition;
  - able to listen and engage constructively with such differences;
- is capable of allowing a curate or student minister to develop in ways different from his/her own with regard to:

  - the deployment of special gifts of ministry;
  - specific delegated responsibilities;
  - being open to styles of mission and pastoral ministry which may be different to his/her own preference;
  - is prepared to put considerable effort into mobilising available resources for the training of a student minister or curate, some of which will lie outside the parish or pastorate;
  - is prepared to give the available post-ordination training and CME programme a high priority and is willing to work with the CME advisor;
  - is able to share ministry with a colleague (including sharing difficulties as well as successes) and to model a collaborative approach to ministry which enables the whole people of God to grow in ministry.

Alongside this list of specifications that a supervisor could be expected to offer, the expectations of the student minister were also outlined. They should have a growing awareness and understanding of the process of learning, and should be increasingly able to evaluate their strengths and weaknesses and their needs for future and continuing development and growth.

This process of growth and learning should be evident across the whole continuum of training for ministry, as was emphasized in *Mission and Ministry* (2003). This report made explicit the aim of theological education, which was to enable the ongoing formation of the minister as someone who could interpret the traditions and scripture in changing situations, drawing strength from the church and able to represent the church in the world. It saluted ACCM 22 for introducing a coherent and considered rationale where before there had been 'chaos' (p. v), and drew attention again to the importance of a theological underpinning to education, lifelong learning and engagement with the world. It offered a review of ecumenical developments, of the development of collaborative styles of ministry and leadership and the diverse ways in which ordained ministry was by then expressed.

By 2003 the Church of England was demanding different things of theological education. As well as calls for more time to be given to traditional theological disciplines, other issues had emerged: mission and evangelism; issues of discrimination (especially 'race', gender and disability); leadership and parochial management; homiletics and contemporary approaches to communication. Increasingly, theological education happened in partnership with universities and with other denominations. Regional groups of institutions had emerged, and local ministry schemes had seen sustained growth. Theological education was, by 2003, attentive to the need for balance and integration between the different disciplines of theology and mindful of the importance of educational method and questions of how theological study contributed to the task of ministry and vice versa. There was now much more clarity about the qualities and competencies desirable in ministers, who needed to be 'creative and flexible in the exercise of their ministry' (p. 41), based upon these three parameters:

- **Interpretation of the Christian Tradition for today**
  Any programme must provide a *deep and intelligent enquiry into the Christian Scripture and Tradition while also relating that to present circumstances* so that such enquiry serves the goal of *discovering the form of God's creative and redemptive activity in the world and learning to participate in it in the present.*
- **The Formation of Church Life:**
  Any programme must provide a *deep enquiry into the conditions of the Churches' life as called by Jesus Christ and living from the energy of the Holy Spirit.*
- **Addressing Situations in the World:**
  Any programme must enable ordinands *to identify the situations in which the Church is formed and to which it must address itself.* (p. 24, emphasis in original)

The authors found, against some opposing opinion, that 'where diversity, creativity and integration have been achieved, this has not entailed the loss of any of the traditional disciplines' (p. 37), and that the skills of reflection and thought needed encouragement to ensure greater continuity in training and lifelong learning.

By the time the 'Hind Report' was published in 2003 the very title incorporates the ground that had been covered since ACCM 22. Properly entitled *Formation for Ministry within a Learning Church*, this report offered radical proposals to resource the church as a community of faith that continued to learn. It proposed the creation of regional training centres so that colleges and courses collaborated with universities to 'provide high-quality training for the clergy that will equip them to offer vibrant and collaborative spiritual leadership and to empower a vocationally motivated laity – and thereby, to promote and serve God's mission in the world' (p. 2).

Formation is seen as a whole process which

seems to us to be required by our belief in the living God who is constantly drawing us deeper into the mystery of Christ. It is also demanded by the exigencies of a rapidly changing world. The ability of the Church to serve the mission of God does not depend on the clergy alone, of course, but their role is crucial and we believe that the work of Christian apologetics as well as of social engagement requires ministers who are versatile and equipped to 'read the signs of the times' (p. 2).

To strengthen the time of initial training, the Hind Report recommends that initial ministerial education be reconfigured as the period from entry into training to the end of the first training post, and it focuses more on the role of supervisor (or training incumbent) than any previous report, recognizing that up to now they 'have worked in a vacuum in terms of national policy', and stating that 'it will be vital that training incumbents are seen as key figures and partners in the continuing ministerial development of the newly ordained, and that the current best practice in their training and development is identified and becomes the standard for all' (p. 45).

In the documents of the Church of England we see how a much more explicit and coherent educational policy reflects the changes in education that I noted at the beginning of the chapter, with the growing emergence of the idea of 'lifelong learning', and with it, methods of reflective practice. I took the Anglican Church as a case study, but many of the same developments have occurred in other denominations and in academic fields where questions of method and context gain increasing recognition in the study of theology.

Alongside the necessity for a firm theological basis to the churches' provision of theological education, there has been a growing appreciation of the ways in which adults learn by holding a balance between academic study and personal development. The reports emphasize knowing, doing and being, held in creative balance or tension, suggesting a holistic approach to the person of the minister. They advocate the fostering of habits of learning that can ensure that theological education is a lifelong commitment. Didactic 'banking' methods give way, or at least are supplemented, by an understanding of learning as a process, where knowledge is understood more as a cognitive map or net where different strands can be developed and pursued. Learning becomes increasingly the responsibility of the learner, with encouragement for learners to evaluate their own needs and objectives with the guidance and oversight of tutor and supervisor. The role of the supervisor emerges as increasingly important, although little is offered to suggest what the role is, nor is there much exploration of how supervision can support processes of lifelong learning beyond the initial training period.

Look back over the six stories of ministry that Geoff, Jean, Roger, Lynn, James and Ben wrote. What would have best served them, in terms of initial training, given the ministries they now provide?

Theological Education: Reflection on Experience: The Portfolio as Method

The Church of England documents that we have examined here mark a shift of emphasis from a creation and redemption model of engagement with the world to a Trinitarian understanding of the minister as 'in relation' with the world, able to reflect upon their practice in diverse contexts. Jackie, when she started her curacy, was required to keep a portfolio during her training experience. In it she kept a variety of reflections and impressions of her first years in ministry, including retrospective material from her time at theological college and placement work. Her participation in a tutor group during the first three years of her Anglican curacy was recorded by reports from tutors, her training incumbent and the Continuing Ministerial Education officer in the diocese. She was asked to write about what she had learned, following the aims and objectives identified for her first three years, including areas of general expertise, personal development, conduct of worship, preaching, pastoral and educational ministry, mission and evangelism, links with the wider church, parochial and personal skills and skills for occasional ministry. She was asked to discern her learning goals for the year, and gather evidence during the year to support her comments. The evidence that Jackie provided included poetry, sermons she had given, books she had read, and accounts of pastoral visits and engagement with community organizations. Alongside these texts, Jackie offered reflections on how she discerned her development in terms of her spirituality, her understanding of her role as a minister, and how she balanced her personal and professional life.

One of her learning goals was 'Conducting Funerals in a Wide Range of Circumstances'. Jackie included orders of service, eulogies and other literature such as appreciation cards as evidence, and wrote the following in evaluation:

Start level 2, target level 4

Where I began . . .

My starting point was level 2 (beginning to learn) as I had, sadly, had a lot of personal experience of funerals and taking part in them. As part of my summer placement through college I had spent some time abroad and this had included time with a Funeral Director. I was familiar with the liturgy and had had some 'bad' experiences to draw upon as well.

Although moving two levels was a lot, there were two main reasons for this goal:

- It's an area of interest for me.
- I knew that Funeral Ministry was a significant part of the ministry of St Paul's and that this was an area in which my incumbent had extensive experience, on which I would be able to draw over the year.

Where am I now?

There is no doubt that the year has brought with it much funeral experience, ranging from the so-called straight-forward to the more difficult family situations and untimely deaths. I was willing to take on board this aspect of ministry more independently very early on and now feel mostly confident in this area (I have also had ample opportunity for both coaching sessions and reflection time with my incumbent in this area). I have had the opportunity to work closely with all the main funeral directors in the area and also conduct funerals in other churches within the Deanery, and the funeral of someone who was known personally to me.

From an initial position of mirroring the funerals that I observed from my incumbent, I have now felt able to develop slightly different ways of working and drawing upon other resources for use at a funeral service. I have received much positive feedback and appreciation from bereaved families – both directly to myself, through my incumbent and through other members of the church and wider community, which has been both encouraging and affirming.

I am more aware than ever of the pastoral implications of Funeral Ministry and the frustrations of finding suitable ways of conducting follow-up – although there is at least one new member of the congregation and Lunch Club as a result of follow-up to his wife's funeral that I had conducted.

Overall, I believe that I have achieved level 4 in this learning goal, although this will now require further consolidation and development with a wider range of situations as they arise. I feel confident to take on the range of funerals if my incumbent is away from the parish and am able to liaise independently with funeral directors as necessary. I would also like, in the future, to develop this area beyond level 4, and this would tie in with my wider interest in both Hospice Ministry and on-going bereavement care.

The diocese in which Jackie started her curacy had a well developed portfolio method of enabling curates to reflect upon their learning experience, to supplement and structure the supervision offered by training incumbents.

The Diocese of Coventry write this about portfolios in their handbook for the first three years of Ministry (June 2002):

Portfolio in CME 1–3

Portfolio is not an end in itself; it is a means to an end. It attempts to bring closer together the CME 1–3 programme and the experience of ministry under supervision, so that all involved can work in partnership towards these ends. It seeks to lay a basis for lifelong learning that will underpin all your ministry.

What is Portfolio?

Whether you are an investor in the stock market, an artist, or in education you will recognize the term portfolio. In CME 1–3 it is an organized collection of things you have been learning. Just as an artist's portfolio shows what kind of artist you are, so a learner's portfolio shows what you have learned. In other words it is a collection of pieces of evidence that shows that learning has really been achieved. It may contain, for example, exam results, or a description of piece of ministry, or feedback from colleagues.

Portfolio is a method of approaching continuous personal and professional development that combines elements of a journal, a learning log and curriculum vitae. The great strength of portfolio is that it focuses both on the development needs of individual people and on the requirement of the organization (in this case, the Church) that people should be effective in the role they occupy.

Portfolio values the whole person and helps you to

integrate different aspects of your life – the emotional, spiritual, intellectual, personal, social and practical aspects of your development. Being an ordained minister implies bringing relevant skills, attitudes and knowledge to ministry in the local and contemporary situation. Continuing Ministerial Education in the first three years should build and encourage on-going participation in the cycle of learning:

Taking action > reflecting > bringing ideas together > applying new learning > taking action >

Portfolio has the potential to deliver clear goals for practical benefits from learning.

What are the benefits and drawbacks of this method of reflection upon learning in practice, do you think?

3

LEARNING TO PLAY:
THE INTERPLAY OF THEOLOGY

In Chapter 1 we explored the ways in which we can learn to 'read the signs of the times', looking at trends in social and global analysis to answer the question, 'What sort of ministry/ ministers do we require for today's church?' With the stories of the six ministers as illustration, I argued that in order for the church to be able to respond to a changing world it requires a flexible and adaptable ministry that is rooted creatively in its living traditions, is socially and politically discerning, able to engage in dialogue with others in diverse contexts and live with ambiguity and uncertainty.

The last chapter showed how educational theory and practice have led to the development within ministerial training and 'formation' of methods of reflective practice and, increasingly, the recognition of the importance of supervision as an educational resource.

This chapter seeks to lay some theological foundations to the practice of supervision within lifelong learning. I am going to begin by exploring some of the ways in which supervision can be understood, and work with different theological aspects that those different ways might suggest. For example, the word 'supervision' etymologically means 'oversight', and might suggest an understanding of a supervisor who continually watches over those who are supervised. Although there is some sense in which 'oversight' is an important element in good supervision, if this metaphor is adopted as the sole model it could lead to the characterization of a supervisor who continually breathes down the neck of the poor reflective practitioner, watching over him or her like a hawk from a great height of superior expertise.

I want, instead, to use the metaphor of 'space', rather than 'sight', to carry forward a way of thinking about supervision. The 'space of supervision' then becomes a space in which mutual learning occurs, a space of interaction and dialogue, a space where identities are formed and transformed, a space of interplay, of experimentation. This space will be employed differently if it is called supervision, or mentoring, or consultancy, or even spiritual direction, but basically what is provided is time and 'space' where both supervisor and reflective practitioner can experience safety and challenge so that growth and learning occurs.

Supervision: The Space to Play

To think of supervision in terms of 'space' is to draw upon the work of D. W. Winnicott, the paediatrician and psychoanalyst who wrote in *Playing and Reality* (1971/1999) of the need for a 'facilitating environment' in which the child could grow and mature. Winnicott described this environment as a space in which the child could take risks in play and exploration within the safe boundaries established and sustained by the 'good-enough' parent. Although childhood was his main focus, he wrote about how adults needed to continue to play, and he understood culture and religion predominantly as offering the space, the 'playground', for this to happen. Winnicott wrote of the 'good-enough mother' as someone who was able to hold the boundaries and take responsibility for the creative possibilities and safety of the space. Many current writers on supervision base their thinking on how Winnicott stressed the importance of safe space to play in learning and development (see, for example, Hawkins and Shohet, 2002, pp. 3ff.; Shipton, 1997, p. 73; Carroll and Throlstrup, 2001, p. 24; Foskett and Lyall, 1990, p. 114).

Winnicott's ideas on the seriousness of play and playing are worth exploring further at this stage. His observations of small children led him to see play as an activity that enabled a child to engage with external reality and, in the right facilitating environment, to experiment and explore their sense of self in the world. As the child developed away from the magic years, when he or she lived with a normal illusion of omnipotence and control, towards a growing realization that relating with others means you do not get your own way all the time, Winnicott thought that an intermediate space where play happened was essential. Deprived of the opportunity to play, the child develops into an adult who is incapable of accepting difference and similarity (1999, p. 6), and who lacks the ability to be creative and engage culturally which includes, for Winnicott, artistic and religious activity. He writes: 'Cultural experience begins with creative living first manifested in play' (p. 100).

But what is play? Play involves the engagement with others, often initially with objects like toys and teddy bears, and then increasingly with people. Play brings together the imaginative life of the child with a growing sense of the reality of the world. Winnicott thinks that the child learns to test out their experience of an inner reality and external life by playing at the boundaries of self and other. A child will draw, and use string which is 'simultaneously a symbol of separateness and of union through communication' (p. 43) and other objects to make sense of their development from total attachment to the mother to the healthy state of being able to negotiate in the world with different perspectives. Often crucial in this negotiation is the part played by transitional objects – a teddy bear (and he describes Winnie-the-Pooh as a classic example), or a comforter, or a thumb that is sucked – which enables the child to engage seriously with the business of growing away from primary attachments towards healthy adulthood. When no longer needed, a transitional object is 'not forgotten and it is not mourned. It loses meaning' (p. 5). But the process that it represents is not lost: the transitional object becomes the basis of the plaything of the adult – the objects and symbols of the cultural life.

Winnicott writes:

> I have used the term cultural experience as an extension of the idea of transitional phenomena and of play without being certain that I can define the word 'culture'. The accent indeed is on experience. In using the word culture I am thinking of the inherited tradition. I am thinking of something that is in the common pool of humanity, into which individuals and groups of people may contribute, and from which we may all draw *if we have somewhere to put what we find*. (p. 99, his emphasis)

He uses the term 'culture' very widely here, as including the wealth of human experience into which a child is initiated and develops. It is all that gives meaning to existence; it is the inherited experience into which someone is born and for Winnicott it includes art, yes, but also religious faith and practice, politics and the social fabric of life. Cultural life is where adults are creative, and for Winnicott, as with play, creativity is universal: 'It belongs to being alive' (p. 67).

'It belongs to being alive'. What are the ways in which you 'play'?

Some 'play' will be simply relaxation – watching the television, for example. Other 'play' will give meaning to your existence by helping you to interpret your experience – going to a concert, or the theatre, for example. Think of a recent time in which you have 'played' and have also learned more about your life and/or ministry as a result.

A healthy child, then, learns through playing to negotiate the me and the not-me and grow into an adult who can creatively handle difference and similarity, and who, indeed, continues to play, using the symbols and artefacts of the inherited cultural tradition in the enjoyment and exploration of life. In psychotherapy, play is crucial: 'it takes place in the overlap of two areas of playing, that of the patient and that of the therapist'. When the client is unable to play, having never learned to do so, 'then the work done by the therapist is directed towards bringing the patient from a state of not being able to play into a state of being able to play' (p. 38). Play is essential to enable the client to explore different options, different possibilities in the search for self – and it is the responsibility of the therapist to create the space for this to happen.

The metaphor of the *space* to play runs through Winnicott's writing. He says 'In order to give a place to playing I postulated a *potential space* between the baby and the mother' (p. 41, his emphasis). This is an intermediate space, a playground, an area which exists outside the individual but which is where the preoccupations of the inner or personal reality are played out. It needs to be a safe place, where the play is not constrained and is able to be spontaneous, not compliant or acquiescent. And then, in this space, the child is able to take risks and enter places which are exciting, and even precarious (p. 51). There needs to be 'good-enough environmental provision' to enable play to occur.

Adulthood, by extension, makes use of this 'potential space', but now it is the space between the individual and the environment (p. 100). He writes:

The potential space between baby and mother, between child and family, between individual and society or the world, depends on experience which leads to trust. It can be looked upon as sacred to the individual in that it is here that the individual experiences creative living. (p. 103)

Both Geoff and Roger described how they spent time with friends during their days and time off. Using your imagination, allow yourself to dream about the space that you retreat to when you need to rest, or to work something out or be creative. Does the space have others there too? Or are you alone?

Using colour, paint or draw a picture of where you go.

The space that Winnicott describes is full of potential for playful explorations into the ground that this book covers. Again and again Winnicott uses the word 'interplay', to refer to the interplay between mother and child; between inner and outer; between attachment and independence. For him it designates a creative tension between different states, different objects, different persons that, like a paradox, is not resolved, but accepted and tolerated, and then 'has value for every human individual who is not only alive and living in this world but who is also capable of being infinitely enriched by exploitation of the cultural link with the past and with the future' p. xii). This metaphorical space is at the heart of this book as a playground where different explorations can happen.

It is an idea that others have developed. Gillie Bolton, in her book *Reflective Practice*, writes of serious playfulness and its importance when dealing with uncertainty:

The only way to make this uncertainty dynamic is by being playful and willing to try a range of things: accepting reflective practice as a process of looking for something when you don't know what it is. An adventurous spirit leads onto that trackless moorland which education has come to be, rather than a walled or hedged field, and discover some pertinent questions. Sacred positions are not taken seriously here: anything and everything is brought into question – even ourselves – leaving no room for self-importance. There is, however, only so much we can do to alter our own situation, that of others, and the wider political one, by reflexivity, reflection, or education: our power is unlimitedly limited.

This playfulness is essentially serious: we are talking professional and personal development, not Ludo. (2003, p. 33)

Winnicott's imaginative and influential thinking can enable us
to understand supervision primarily as an educational process
in which the one responsible for the learning does indeed have
the task of 'watching over' the processes of growth. Much
as a 'good-enough' parent will watch over a child at play, a
supervisor holds the space in which someone else, or a group,
is able to experiment and reflect with what is uncertain and to
play with their practice. So there is a sense in which supervision as oversight is important, but following Winnicott the
emphasis is much more upon overseeing the creation of a good
facilitating environment with clear boundaries rather than a
supervisor who directs learning because she or he has all the
answers. The model of supervision that is used here stresses
the mutuality of learning and the sharing of experience within
a space where boundaries are held primarily by the supervisor. Although at times there will inevitably be a need for
assessment or appraisal, the main emphasis is on gaining skills
in reflection upon practice, skills which are 'owned' by the
learners.

As Moon has argued, if appraisal or assessment is to be
effective in terms of changing practice, it needs to be 'owned'
in a similar way, and can be incorporated within the safety
and challenge of the space that supervision provides to play
and experiment (2004, p. 149). Supervision needs to include
the opportunity to reflect and assess oneself, much as Jackie
did in her portfolio which was then to be discussed with her
supervisor. This enhances the learning itself.

At the heart of good supervision is the encounter between
the supervisor and reflective practitioner (whether one-to-one
or in a group). This encounter at its best will foster mutual
trust and a growing understanding that enables challenging
learning opportunities to be embraced. For such an encounter
to occur there needs to be structure and an agreed regularity
of meeting. There needs to be the willingness, certainly on the

part of the supervisor, to be open and encouraging, to discern and work with their own defensiveness at times, and appreciate and respect the ways in which the reflective practitioner may struggle to share a sense of failure and vulnerability and have well constructed defences in place. Learning often best happens when insight is reached through struggling with what has *not* worked in practice, when we are able to return to what we think of as failure. To provide an environment that facilitates such learning, the supervisor needs to be able to give of herself, to be generous and trustworthy.

Winnicott's central idea of the space to play as essential for growth and learning to occur resonates with ways in which 'space' can be understood more theologically. John V. Taylor's book *The Go-Between God* is well worth rereading for the insights he gives into the working of the Holy Spirit in the space between people. I use also the work of Miroslav Volf, a Croatian theologian now working in the United States, who has written on identity, otherness and reconciliation. Although he is mainly concerned with dialogue in the face of seemingly irreconcilable cultural difference, his reflections upon the nature of the Trinity and differentiation give theological enrichment to the interplay of supervision. Emmanuel Levinas' understanding of a welcome to the other that goes beyond what might be expected is helpful. Levinas puts self-giving and generosity at the heart of encounter, and to take this generosity into supervision is to realize it as an expansive space that embraces the potential of a wide diversity of material from the reflective practitioner's ministry. We look briefly also at Julia Kristeva's writing on how important it is to recognize 'the stranger' within our own identity. These thinkers provide a depth of reflection which can enrich the experience of supervision.

Supervision that nurtures playful dialogue and exploration enables learning about the material brought for exploration. Learning also happens implicitly. The reflective practitioner learns skills of listening and reflecting by watching and experiencing the supervisor in action. This process of 'modelling' is especially important when we consider how important dialogue is in the diverse contexts in which ministry is practised in today's world. The ability of the supervisor to enable different opinions to be expressed and avenues to be explored becomes important learning in itself, and will be replicated in other places and with other people by the reflective practitioner. The ability to understand difference and work with diversity is often largely gained as the reflective practitioner experiences how his own differences are respected and worked with in supervision.

> Think of an example from your own experience where you have 'picked up' good habits from observing someone else's practice. Then think of a time when you have 'picked up' bad habits.

The Go-Between God

The way in which the minister relates to others – the interplay – is central to ministry. To reflect theologically upon that is to consider how God relates and is active in the world. In 1972 John V. Taylor wrote *The Go-Between God*. It reads now as a product of its age: bold in its liberal outlook, non-inclusive in its language. But as a book it stands the test of time, not least in the way Taylor portrays the Holy Spirit as enabling truthful encounter with difference, and intimately concerned with the difficult task of living with diversity in today's world. Taylor bemoans the lack of attention that the Holy Spirit had received in theological circles at the time he was writing, 'relegated to the merest edges of our theology' (p. 5). He develops the idea of God as there on the inside of human relating, undergirding the ways in which relatedness between self and other is carried forward without collapsing otherness into the self:

My spirit, therefore, is never uniquely mine as are my body, my life, my individuality. It resides only in my relatedness to some other. Spirit is that which lies between making both separateness and conjunction real. (p. 8)

Taylor describes God the Holy Spirit as 'the beyond in the midst' (p. 5). The go-between God is intimately concerned with the complexities, joys and difficulties of human relating, fully in the midst of the interplay of encounter. Whatever is encountered, whether it be an object or another human being, is encountered face to face: 'for now this other being meets me in its own authenticity, and I am face to face with the truth *of* it, not merely the truth *about* it' (pp. 12–13, his emphasis). Taylor describes such encounters with otherness as 'annunciations' (p. 10), moments of truth between self and other that do not deny the radical and absolute nature of otherness. The God who is 'beyond in the midst' enables the truth of the giving that occurs in such an encounter: 'in these moments of mutual awareness, the other demands that I be truly myself, it demands also that I be all that I am capable of being. There is nothing inert or passive about the mutual giving: it is intense and exacting . . . Real listening and real looking takes it out of one, though one only becomes conscious of this afterwards' (p. 15).

When was the last time that someone really listened to you? Write down what you think the qualities were that made this an intense and exacting 'mutual giving'.

The go-between God is to be discerned exactly in such encounters, when self cannot fail to be moved by the truth of the other which addresses the self and calls for a response that draws the person out of himself, thus creating a fellowship based upon mutual giving and recognition. This "is 'the Communion'", the in-between-ness, of the Holy Spirit . . . what causes the fellowship is the gift of awareness which opens our eyes to one another, makes us see as we never saw before' (p. 17). The presence of God is to be discerned here, in the space of encounter.

This space in which learning comes from interplay and

exploration is precisely what is so important to supervision. Perhaps the icon of Rublev was in Taylor's mind when he wrote:

> Every time I am given this unexpected awareness towards some other creature and feel this current of communication between us, I am touched and activated by something that comes from the fiery heart of the divine love, the eternal gaze of the Father towards the Son, of the Son towards the Father . . . The first essential activity of the Spirit is annunciation. It is always he who gives one to the other and makes each really see the other. (p. 18)

The Trinity can be thought in terms of 'perichoresis' – 'dancing around' – a word that describes a dance that sustains distance in intimate connection and is a way of understanding God's activity in relationship both between the persons of the Trinity and with the world. In recent years, many writers have returned to this concept of perichoresis, an interest anticipated by Taylor. The go-between God suggests the way the Holy Spirit is found in the go-between spaces of the dance. It is a fruitful image to enrich the way we think of the space of supervision as a place in which God sustains the reflection and the playful experimentation of learning.

Taylor notes another function of the Holy Spirit: to open eyes and minds. He writes:

> The Holy Spirit is the invisible third party who stands between me and the other, making us mutually aware. Supremely and primarily he opens my eyes to Christ. But he also opens my eyes to the brother in Christ, or the fellowman, or the point of need, or the heartbreaking brutality and the equally heartbreaking beauty of the world. He is the giver of that vision without which the people perish. We so commonly speak about him as the source of *power*. But in fact he enables us not by making us supernaturally strong but by opening our eyes.
>
> The Holy Spirit is that power which opens eyes that are

closed, hearts that are unaware and minds that shrink from too much reality. If one is open towards God, one is open also to the beauty of the world, the truth of ideas, and the pain of disappointment and deformity. If one is closed up against being hurt, or blind towards one's fellow-men, one is inevitably shut off from God also. One cannot choose to be open in one direction and closed in another. Vision and vulnerability go together. Insensitivity is also an all-rounder. If for one reason or another we refuse really to *see* another person, we become incapable of sensing the presence of God. (p. 19, his emphasis)

It might seem that this God who is the beyond-in-the-midst is only ever present when the face-to-face encounter is infused with annunciation and mutual recognition. Taylor does touch upon the necessity for dialogue to 'probe beyond the glad discovery of similarities to the more painful recognition of differences that are mutually exclusive' (p. 186). Perhaps more so in today's world than Taylor realized we face real difficulties of dialogue. Seemingly insurmountable differences of culture and religious practice perplex theologians and social and cultural commentators alike. But the crucial point that Taylor makes is that dialogue will often remain with the unfathomable difficulties of difference unless the otherness of the beyond is recognized as a crucial element in carrying forward any dialogue: 'to stop at the disagreements is to lose faith in the Spirit's gift of communion and communication' (p. 187).

It is the generosity of Taylor's go-between God that is attractive here: the sense in which with such a God it is possible to go the extra step that makes dialogue work.

I have already remarked on how Levinas too puts generosity at the heart of his ethic of human relating. It is the 'après vous' injunction that has its roots deep within Jewish texts that Levinas develops as he explores radical difference or 'alterity', a word that has come to be associated with his writing. Only if we are able to extend ourselves towards the other, to the extent, Levinas says, of placing ourselves in their position, can we begin to communicate across the gulf of otherness. This becomes important both within the relationship of supervisor and reflective practitioner, but also, in a parallel way, in the work of ministry. There is required in ministry, and in supervision, the sort of kenosis that Levinas advocates so that we can grow and develop.

A World of Difference

Though Taylor doesn't mention Levinas, Miroslav Volf does. His book *Exclusion and Embrace* (1996) is the fruit of his reflections upon cultural conflict. Volf is a Croatian Christian who now lives in Los Angeles. He describes himself as 'a child of a "mixed marriage", I have Czech, German, and Croatian "blood" in my veins; I grew up in a city which the old Hapsburg Empire had made into a meeting place of many ethnic groups. And I live in the (tension-filled) multicultural city of Los Angeles' (p. 16). From his experience of the war in the former Yugoslavia, and observations of various other kinds of cultural 'cleansings' he argues that it is crucial '*to place identity and otherness at the center of theological reflection* on social realities' (p. 17, his emphasis). He explores the ways in which the dyad 'us and them' comes to be constructed and how peoples can exclude others, even to death. He counters 'exclusion' with 'embrace'. Embrace can be profoundly difficult, but is the only response possible in the face of the evils of exclusion.

At worst, exclusion is born of the 'need to control and the discomfort with internal and external "dirt"' (p. 79). But why, he asks, 'Why do we want to control everything alone instead of sharing our possessions and power, and making space for others in a common household? Why do others strike us as "dirt" rather than "ornament"? Why cannot we accept our shadows so as to be able to embrace others instead of projecting our own unwanted evil onto them?' (p. 79). The relationship between self and other is fundamental to identity.

For Volf, a defensive self, unable to integrate its own 'dirt', is liable to be unable to dialogue or to embrace the other. But self and other belong together, he argues: without 'others' we can have no sense of self: 'the formation and negotiation of identity always entails the drawing of boundaries, the setting of the self as distinct from the other' (p. 90). But it is necessary to be able to take the other into oneself, and here he acknowledges his debt to Levinas. He writes profoundly, I think, of the need for embrace that becomes a profound encounter with the other, changing both in the process:

> The tendency towards violence is, moreover, reinforced by an inescapable ambiguity of the self. The self is dialogically constructed. The other is already from the outset part of the self. I am who I am in relation to the other; to be Croat is, among other things, to have Serbs as neighbors; to be white in the U.S. is to enter a whole history of relation to African Americans (even if you are a recent immigrant). Hence the will to be oneself, if it is to be healthy, must entail the will to let the other inhabit the self; the other must be part of who I am as I will to be myself. As a result, a tension between the self and the other is built into the very desire for identity: the other over against whom I must assert myself is the same other who must remain part of myself if I am to be myself. But the other is often not the way I want her to be (say, she is aggressive or simply more gifted) and is pushing me to become the self that I do not want to be (suffering her incursions or my own inferiority). And yet I must integrate the other into my own will to be myself. Hence I slip into violence: instead of reconfiguring myself to make space for the other, I seek to reshape the other into who I want her to be in order that in relation to her I may be who I want to be. (p. 91)

To embrace the other and not to slip into violence against the other, Volf draws on his understanding of the Triune God when he writes: 'I will argue that reconciliation with the other will succeed only if the self, guided by the narrative of the triune God, is ready to receive the other into itself and undertake a re-adjustment of its identity in light of the other's alterity' (p. 110). The Trinity shows a God who is relation, a relation of love and mutuality. Each requires the other in order to have identity, but none is collapsed into the other. Within the Trinity is relatedness that refuses sameness (God as one) and sustains differentiation between the three persons. This provides the pattern for how God relates to the world, for the world and humanity are embraced:

> When the Trinity turns toward the world, the Son and the Spirit become, in Irenaeus' beautiful image, the two arms of God by which humanity was made and taken into God's embrace . . . That same love that sustains nonself-enclosed identities in the Trinity seeks to make space 'in God' for humanity. (p. 128)

Faced with human otherness even unto enmity, Volf finds here a divine pattern of inclusion and embrace that puts the cross at the centre of divine and human relating, and therefore at the centre of human self and otherness. The embrace of the other, even one's enemy, is the commandment for those who seek to follow Christ, and such embrace requires self-emptying, kenosis; a reaching out in generosity and love to the other, so that the other can find space to be.

Volf's thinking finds an echo in the work of another philosopher who has reflected upon identity and difference. Julia Kristeva explores the way in which the reality of global mobility can instil the need to incorporate strangeness within oneself, so that always the subject carries internally a sense of otherness. She arrived in 1966 in Paris from Bulgaria to take up a doctoral fellowship. She was fluent in Russian, and took the Parisian intellectual scene by storm. Always a foreigner, she argued that the state of translation is the common condition of all thinking beings. Language for her is the process of constant translation and adaptation to different cultural realities, and indeed to be able to write at all, you need to become a stranger to your own country, language, sex and identity. In *Strangers to Ourselves* (1991) she helps us to encounter the otherness of strangers, by drawing attention to the strangers that is within. Our sense of identity is not unitary, but made up of many different elements, different roles that we play, different sides to our personality. To incorporate a sense of alienation within ourselves is to recognize the experience of being alien in community today, where 'community' can be little more than a romantic myth (see Smith, 1996, for further reading). Both she and Volf speak of a world in which fragmentation and displacement have become, or are in the process of becoming, the norm. For Kristeva, to embrace the stranger in oneself can be to open up new patterns of creativity and new possibilities for action in the world.

With these thinkers we have a way of reflecting upon the space in which the encounter of supervision happens and a way of thinking of the relationship between supervisor and reflective practitioner (whether individual or group) as one that can be modelled on the sustained differentiation that is to be found within the Trinity. The metaphor of perichoresis suggests a dynamic relating, a dance of dialogue and mutual exploration as reflective practitioner and supervisor are formed and transformed in the quest to understand each other. The material that is brought for reflection becomes a rich elaboration, exploration and interplay of self and different others encountered in the world of ministry.

Supervision: The Space of Interplay

Taylor and Volf offer theological reflections that take us further in our consideration of supervision as a space of play and interplay. The word 'interplay' recognizes the need for the other in the formation and transformation of the self. In my dictionary it is defined as 'reciprocal action; operation of two things on each other'. It encapsulates well, I think, the relationship of a reflective practitioner and supervisor. It does not suggest too heavy a didactic teaching model, but rather a mutuality of learning. Volf's use of the metaphor of 'embrace' captures something similar of the risk of encountering difference. So supervision as interplay, a time of serious play in which the encounter between self and other partakes of the dynamic of a Trinitarian God; a rich and playful pursuit which is complex and dialogical.

And where is God? Another voice in the dialogue? Perhaps. Or perhaps it is God who holds the metaphorical space in which we live and move and have our being. A God who is 'good-enough' (to use Winnicott's memorable phrase) to enable us to live creatively. Who holds the deep resonances of our dialogues. The space of supervision can be understood as a space of creative complexity, perhaps like a symphony, or to return to the image of the Introduction, an enormous hammock or safety net, as different strands of the narratives of different lives come together.

> The front cover of this book shows the image of a tree trunk that has been worn and cracked by weather. The sunshine and shadows contribute to the texture. In what ways does it 'work' as an image for the content of this book? Are there other images you would chose to suggest the presence of God in the practice of supervision?

We have explored how the space of supervision can provide the opportunity for a playful encounter with otherness, with difference. The supervisor does not look on in a disinterested or superior way, but does have oversight for establishing the boundaries and the creation of a good-enough facilitating environment for learning. Much of the learning that is formative of self and identity will be as a result of the engagement with alterity or difference, an engagement that is at the heart of ministry. To dialogue well with difference is perhaps one of the most important skills for a minister in today's world. In supervision such skills can be learned and developed as the reflective practitioner brings the other spaces and times of their work in communities, in different contexts and different practices. The interplay of supervision becomes a constant interaction between different others, a dynamic interplay of standpoint, of dialogue, of power, of difference.

4

LEARNING TO LISTEN: THE PRACTICE OF SUPERVISION

In the last chapter we explored the metaphor of the 'space' of supervision, a facilitating environment where experimentation with practice can happen, risks be taken, dialogue be heard and creative options can be tried out. If supervision is to be a space where different tensions and challenges can be held in safety, it is most important that clear contracts are drawn up from the beginning, and a robust interpretative framework is employed to contain and then make sense of the discomfort that new learning can provoke. The agreement together of a contract at the beginning of the process of supervision makes the exercise mutual, and sets the pattern for a quality of listening that the reflective practitioner should be able to expect from the supervisor.

Making the Contract

Whether supervision is one-to-one or in a group, establishing a contract is an essential part of creating and sustaining a sense of safety in supervision. Hawkins and Shohet outline five areas that need to be covered: the practicalities, boundaries, working alliance, the session format, the organizational and professional context (2002, p. 54).

'Practicalities' includes all the practical arrangements such as frequency of meeting, place, how long, what might be allowed to interrupt or postpone the session, clarity about any payment that is involved. Depending on whether this is group supervision or one-to-one, such practicalities will differ. What is important is that they are agreed before or at the first session. For someone who is in the middle of describing a sensitive area of work to a supervisor, to find themselves interrupted by a phone conversation, and then 'where were we?' from the supervisor jeopardizes the environment of learning and reflecting. Merely knowing that such interruptions are a possibility prevents, on the reflective practitioner's part, the risk of further levels of engagement. It is important to recognize that the supervisor's ability to establish clarity about practicalities, and to keep to them, offers a model of learning in itself. Neil Burgess, in *Into Deep Water*, offers many examples of poor practice here. One curate commented

> He's always late for Morning Prayer and I find that very difficult to handle . . . We don't have regular staff meetings at regular times; a professional relationship is lacking . . . we don't work together . . . It makes it very difficult for me to respect him. . . . He doesn't give me any time; [because] he's always late there isn't any space . . . In a staff meeting . . . if someone rings up he won't sit down and [attend to what we are doing]. (1998, pp. 78–9)

Reflect upon your experience of drawing up a contract for supervision. How did you go about clarifying assumptions and setting goals for working together?

Boundaries

The question of boundaries raises the issue of what is appropriate work within a supervision session. Often there can be a real pull towards other business like sorting out preaching rotas, or talking through plans and visiting – properly the work of a staff meeting. Alternatively, supervision can be taken over by various concerns that become counselling, especially if the work itself is challenging and personally difficult. A good way of ensuring that the supervision session remains focused is to ensure that *learning about the work and practice of ministry* is central, rather than organizing the work, or sorting out personal problems. 'What is being learned here about the practice of ministry?' should be a constant question. For example, a difficult funeral visit may stir a number of distressing feelings that need to be owned and explored within supervision. It will be important to explore those feelings in supervision with the recognition that this is to learn about self-awareness in order to minister better in the future, not to provide counselling. Supervision is a learning process, and because it can tackle difficult material, the time together can be easily sidetracked. Some of the more common ways of resisting the work of supervision are found in Chapter 6 below.

Boundaries of confidentiality are necessary, too, as a means of establishing the safety of the space of learning. It is very important to be clear about what might be shared and in what circumstances. The supervisor, for example, may wish to take material to her own supervision, and will need to indicate that this is a possibility at the beginning of a contract. It could be expressed in these terms: 'I am supervising you, and I also receive supervision. There will be times when I will want to discuss our work together with my supervisor. You need to be assured that any material I take from our work will be treated with respect and in confidence. In the supervision I receive, the focus is on *my* role and practice rather than the particularities of *your* situation.' To express it like this also indicates how the reflective practitioner's own work will be handled in supervision – with respect for the situation and in confidence.

Sometimes situations might arise that require information to be taken over the boundary of supervision, for example, if something is disclosed that involves the safety of someone else, if guidelines of pastoral practice have been breached or if a working relationship has so broken down that the organization responsible needs to be aware of the situation. To prevent any sense of betrayal, clarity needs to be there from the outset as to how and to whom information is to be shared. The best option is for the reflective practitioner to take responsibility for sharing the information themselves in the appropriate quarter, in which case the supervisor might say, 'What you have just told me does not only belong here in supervision. You need to take the responsibility of discussing that with X [for example, a tutor, a CME officer].'

Clear assurances that the material of supervision will be treated in a respectful and professional manner should be made. Ensuring that such matters as confidentiality are agreed at the outset contributes to the establishment of a working relationship that will allow potentially difficult material to be expressed and heard within an atmosphere of safety.

The Working Alliance

Hawkins and Shohet write:

> A good working alliance is not built on a list of agree-ments or rules, but on growing trust, respect and good-will between both parties. The contract provides a holding frame in which the relationship can develop, and any lapses in fulfilling the contract need to be seen as opportunities for reflection, learning and relationship building, not judgement and defence. (2002, p. 56)

The purpose of a contract is to allow a relationship of trust and respect to grow. It provides the parameters of safety and challenge, and it helps for the reflective practitioner or group to discuss with the supervisor what expectations they have of supervision. What do the reflective practitioners most want to concentrate upon? Hawkins and Shohet suggest (p. 56) that it can be helpful to complete sentences such as

- 'My image of successful supervision is . . .'
- 'What I fear happening in supervision is . . .'

With a clear understanding of the purpose of the boundaries of the supervision it can become possible to discuss the times when those boundaries are called into question. If the reflective practitioner is late, is this indicative of a reluctance to address an issue? If the conversation strays into chit-chat about the weather, is something more serious being avoided? The working alliance needs to keep its focus upon the practice of ministry. It is the responsibility of the supervisor to ensure that it does and to recall the practitioner or group to the task in hand by naming the ways in which the focus has become blurred. Why and how it becomes blurred can be made a learning opportunity in itself.

> Take the two questions above, and if you are currently receiving or giving supervision, use this opportunity to evaluate what your image of successful supervision is, and what your fears are.

Assessment

Moon argues that with adult learners, assessment is best understood as something that enhances the learning itself, as negotiated within the working relationship. She comments that 'the most obvious way of assessing experiential learning is to ask the learner to demonstrate the ability that the learning has concerned' (2004, p. 150). She argues that assessment is a basic part of the design of reflective or experiential learning, not a separate issue (p. 151) and can be incorporated within the learning contract from the beginning, so that both supervisor and reflective practitioner think about what is learned. She says assessment is for the following reasons:

- for general quality assurance purposes
- to indicate readiness for more advanced study
- to focus learning

- to motivate students to learn
- to shape/direct learning
- to require that students can apply or transfer their learning to unexpected situations.

To work at these goals is to recognize the institutional context which is responsible for the training situation. But it is also to incorporate assessment into the learning contract from the beginning, ensuring that the lifelong learning is focused and owned by the learner and that there is clarity about the roles of supervisor and others who represent the different 'stakeholders' within the learning situation. When the responsibility for the learning is appropriately shared, then when a sense of failure or disappointment is brought to supervision, the emphasis is not so much on the failure itself, as on what can be, or has been, learned from the situation. The freedom to play with alternative strategies, to explore different ways of dealing with a difficult problem, then to assess effectiveness, and be able to transfer learning from one situation to another becomes the business of supervision.

Session Format

So what might be expected within a session of supervision? After exploring hopes and fears of supervision, some expectations of what work is to be done should be aired. The reflective practitioner might bring a case study of a particular incident, or a verbatim report of a visit she has done, recording as far as she can remember, word for word, the conversation she has had with someone. The material brought for supervision will often be because it has stirred the reflective practitioner in some way and left them with questions or a sense of unease about what was said or happened. Some examples are given below.

It may be the case that in a working relationship where supervisor and reflective practitioner work closely together in ministry, that supervision spills over from the session. Conversations about particular aspects of work and learning occur in different times and places as part of ongoing reflection. It can be helpful to recognize that supervision happens in informal ways and in *ad hoc* places, in a creative and spontaneous way. Care should be taken, though, that this is not the *only* way in which supervision happens. The clear boundaries of session work, and therefore more difficult stuff that needs to be tackled, can be lost in such encounters.

The Organizational and Professional Context

The fifth area of work that Hawkins and Shohet highlight is the organizational and professional context (2002, p. 56). Supervision does not happen in a vacuum; more often than not it occurs within a professional setting where an organization – like a church or a hospital, a training course or college – has a stake in what learning occurs in the supervision. This organization will have its own expectations, and in terms of theological education for ministry, many of these expectations are increasingly explicit as guidelines for good practice. It is as well to be aware of the role of the organization and recognize its expectations within supervision, especially in terms of monitoring progress, the acquisition of competencies and assessment. A useful exercise within supervision is to list the people who represent the organization and to whom both supervisor and reflective practitioner feel a sense of accountability for the effectiveness of their work together.

Mapping the Space

Having established clear boundaries that enable supervision to be a focused reflection on practice, it can be useful for the supervisor to have a structure in mind to ensure that he or she holds the potential complexity of the work. Hawkins and

Shohet develop a model that locates supervision within the organizational context, a model they name 'the seven-eyed model of supervision' (2002, p. 68). This model enables them to interpret the many-layered and complex work and processes of supervision, taking into consideration the key players and dynamics between them. Writing for people in helping professions, they focus particularly on the psychodynamic processes of counselling and therapy, and pay attention to the transferences and counter-transferences of supervision, providing a rich resource for understanding the depth and complexity of supervision (pp. 68–87). Foskett and Lyall use a simpler model 'the clinical rhombus' (first developed by Ekstein and Wallerstein, 1972) which is easier to keep in mind. The four points of the rhombus are

A   the reflective practitioner: the person who brings some aspects of practice to supervision;
B   the supervisor;
C   the situation (people, events) that the reflective practitioner seeks to explore;
D   the agency, or institution, or organization that has responsibility for the learning and to which supervisor and reflective practitioner are accountable in terms of delivering good practice in the situation.

This four-pointed figure enables the reflective practitioner and the supervisor to analyse the relationships involved in any given encounter in such a way as the tensions and creative points can be recognized and worked with productively.

    The reflective practitioner is at point A; the supervisor, at point B. The 'situation' is at point C and at the fourth point, D, is the organizational or professional context. This might be a hospital, or church or any other professional or institutional face which is involved and to which the reflective practitioner, the supervisor and the learning are accountable. It can be drawn in this way:

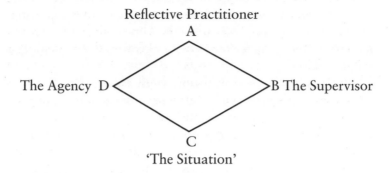

Figure 4: The Clinical Rhombus.

One of the advantages of drawing the training situation in this way is that it enables the reflective practitioner and supervisor to recognize some of the pressures that are at play, including socio-political dynamics and relations of power. With the establishment of a good degree of trust, the reflective practitioner may find her/himself bringing feelings and reflections that are difficult to contain, and often are projected out elsewhere so that they do not have to be faced. To be able to recognize and understand those pressures and projections, and give them a place, mapping them onto the web of the clinical rhombus can help the processes of learning and reflection upon practice.

For example, imagine a reflective practitioner, Alison (A) who visits Mrs Grey (C) and then came to talk with the supervisor (B). Mrs Grey had recently been into hospital and had an awful time with the nurses and no one visited her from the church. So there were two agencies (D) here – the hospital (D1) and the local church (D2), both of which are responsible for some aspects of Mrs Brown's well-being. Alison has come to supervision ill at ease and guilty because Mrs Grey was very depressed. She was feeling cross with the nurses for not having more time for Mrs Grey. A supervisor might then explore the dynamics that occur, using the rhombus as a way of understanding what is happening in this pastoral situation. Alison could be encouraged to see how the two agencies, the church and the hospital, were set up in an unconscious 'splitting' process. It was easier to blame 'the nurses' than to own the uncomfortable guilt feelings and ambivalence that belonged with the church.

Let's look back to Geoff's work with a working party of a local community network. If he were to bring that experience to supervision, and use the rhombus, it might look like this:

At (A) is Geoff, the reflective practitioner. He describes to the supervisor (B) how he is concerned about the 'massive gap between local authority processes and the way in which people relate to what is going on in their community'. It is the work of the working party that he is immediately engaged with, so that belongs at point (C). The working party is frustrated by the local authority consultation process, which is an agency in the situation (D1) and is seeking to represent the voices of 'the community', which is another agency (D2) in the situation that Geoff describes.

Let us assume that Geoff begins to talk through what happened at the meeting, the concerns and frustrations that the Single Regeneration Budget was coming to an end, and the uncertainty of what was to follow as the services provided were reshaped with seemingly little real consultation. Perhaps he would tell his supervisor what was said and by whom, and express something of how the working party explored the ways in which voices of local residents could be heard. In the session, the supervisor might encourage Geoff to explore further the sense of frustration in the situation: who and how it was expressed, and who in particular it was aimed at. The supervisor might identify the 'massive gap' between local people and the local authority processes, and help Geoff (and with him the working party) to explore who exactly the local authority is, and the local people are, so that those two agencies (D1 and D2) might be brought together more directly, thus ensuring that the frustrations felt within the working party became effective in motivating the voices of (D2) to be heard by (D1).

It might well be that the supervisor (B) experiences in this session a sense of frustration as he listens to Geoff's narrative. His previous training and ongoing experience would encourage him to attend to those feelings that he has as important material to reflect upon in helping Geoff to sort through the complexities of the situation.

The Parallel Process

In reflecting upon the feelings stirred within him, this supervisor would be recognizing a dynamic that has been called 'the Parallel Process'. Janet Mattinson was perhaps the first to identify the way in which some tension, or feeling, which initially belonged in the work situation, is carried unconsciously into the supervision setting as unfinished business, as it were. She wrote: 'The thesis is simple. The processes at work in the relationship between client and worker are often reflected in the relationship between worker and supervisor' (quoted in Foskett and Lyall, 1990, p. 130).

For example, if the reflective practitioner appears anxious to please the supervisor, or particularly frustrated, or angry, it can be a useful line of enquiry for the supervisor to trace that anxiety to please, or frustration, back to the situation of ministry that is under consideration. For often it will be the case that the presenting emotion in supervision parallels how the reflective practitioner has handled the original scenario. Moreover the same strong feeling can end up being felt by the supervisor herself. Foskett and Lyall suggest that supervisors, 'by reflecting upon their reactions to those they supervise and the work they hear about, will often become aware of something for which there is no apparent evidence: feelings of anger or boredom, flights of fancy, thoughts and associations. If they can bring these forward and include them in some way, it is likely that they will reveal some of the issues just beneath the surface' (p. 131).

A good example of the parallel process is found in Hawkins

and Shohet as a colleague of theirs, Joan Wilmot, describes it:

> I was supervising a social work student on placement at our therapeutic community who was counselling a resident with whom she was having difficulty. He was a man in his forties who had been in the rehabilitation programme in the house for about seven months and was now to move on to the next stage which was finding himself some voluntary work. He was well able to do this but despite the student making many helpful and supportive suggestions, he 'yes but' everything she said. In her supervision with me, despite her being a very able student, her response to all my interventions was 'yes but'. I took this issue to my supervisor, in order as I thought, to obtain some useful suggestions with which to help the student. However, despite the fact that I was usually very receptive to supervision, I responded to every suggestion my supervisor made with a 'yes but'. He then commented on how resistant I was sounding and how like the resident in question I was being. This insight immediately rang so true that we were both able to enjoy the unconscious paralleling I had been engaged in and I no longer needed to engage in a resistance game with my supervisor. I shared this with my student who no longer needed to resist me but was able to go back to her client and explore his need to resist. His issues around needing to feel his power by resisting could then be worked on separately from his finding voluntary work and he was able to arrange some voluntary work within the week. (2002, p. 81)

The parallel process is a well recognized phenomenon that accounts for the way in which similar responses and behaviour occur in different contexts, and often the main relating factor between these different contexts will be the person who operates in each. For example, the reflective practitioner who is struggling with a reaction to a situation in the context of their work or placement will unconsciously bring the feelings (and behaviours) involved and 'play them out' in the supervision session. Often the group or supervisor will be experience these feelings 'transferred' and attention to such unconscious feelings and naming them can result in valuable learning.

Group Supervision: An Example

This dynamic often happens within groups. As a group works on material that a participant has brought, uncomfortable feelings, which might have started with the participant or the situation they are working with, end up being felt by members of the group. Taking different perspectives and roles identified from the material can be especially valuable in bringing the hidden patterns of responses and behaviours to light.

If we imagine Lynn brought an aspect of her ministry to a supervision session, this time to a peer supervision group of six where one has taken the role of facilitator, it might unfold like this. Lynn describes the conversation that she had in the café about clairvoyance. She wants to explore with her supervision group how they would have responded, and whether her response could have been better. She briefly tells the group about the discussion. If you remember, someone in the café had produced a magazine where the clairvoyant answered a letter that was clearly from one of the people in the parish telling how their son had choked to death in his room, after locking the door. Lynn might outline the direction the conversation took as they sat around the table in the café by writing a verbatim report of what was said. The supervisor of the group could then ask different members of the group to role play what they might have said as if they were sitting there. Such an approach can be very helpful in opening up different perspectives about the situation with the recognition that this is an imaginative exercise, and needs a spirit of openness and a suspension of a literalistic frame of mind to succeed.

Alternatively, the supervisor could ask the group to assume the roles of the clinical rhombus. One might take the perspective of the person (C) who wrote the letter to the clairvoyant, imagining why the letter was written and what need it expressed. Another member of the group might take the perspective of the clairvoyant (D), and two others take the two main perspectives that emerged from the café group itself, as it played around with the ideas of clairvoyance and Christianity. The fifth member of the group (with Lynn sitting silent and listening to what followed) takes the perspective of Lynn herself, the reflective practitioner (A), imagining what Lynn wanted to say, as the minister of the local church. The group might recognize that Lynn was also an agency (D), with feelings of responsibility as the local minister for the family of the son who had died. In role play, each member of the group would try to bring in the different perspectives and issues involved, perhaps drawing out whether Lynn felt uncomfortable about the ministry offered by the clairvoyant that so impressed the café group. Her comment that 'I always have something else to do when these discussions start but they seem to be at the heart of what the café is about' might well have indicated to the peer group that Lynn felt both ambivalent and engaged in the discussion, wanting to encourage such conversations but threatened by the prevalence of different pseudo-religious beliefs. Such discussion within the peer group, undertaken with a lightness of touch and an exploratory approach, could help Lynn and each member of the group to explore further the issues involved in working with people for whom church is relatively strange and alien compared with clairvoyance, and how ministry in a situation where church is marginal can be made more effective. Recognizing the importance of discussions in the café, and Lynn's ambivalence about staying with them when she 'always has something else to do', might be very affirmative feedback that her peer group could give her.

By way of example of how a supervision session might attend to some aspect of ministry brought by a reflective practitioner, we have looked at two of the accounts of ministry and imagined how, typically, a supervisor and a peer group might have explored with Geoff and Lynn these extracts from their writing. To have in one's mind the different perspectives and points of the rhombus can help provide a framework for understanding the dynamics and points of tension and pressure that are present, and can enable the imaginative exploration of different voices so that the reflective practitioner comes away with a deeper grasp of the complexity of ministry and what action might be appropriate in the ongoing practice of ministry.

Verbatim Reports

Clinical Pastoral Education relies upon such detailed attention to particular aspects of a visit, or an interaction with a client on a hospital ward, or encounter with colleague. Within CPE the reflective practitioner will be encouraged to write down verbatim the conversation that occurred and bring it to supervision. That report will become the basis, either within a group or one-to-one, of an exploration of the dynamics of practice, including differentials of power, role and authority.

What is a verbatim report? How does one go about writing them? The rest of this chapter looks at how to

- produce a verbatim report
- read a verbatim report, using examples.

To produce a verbatim report, it is important to

- **listen** closely and attentively to the conversation you are having in any given situation.
  - ○ Listen to yourself – the questions you ask, the comments you make.
  - ○ Listen to his/her/their responses.
  - ○ Listen to the course of the conversation, making a mental note of surprising twists and turns, and of silences.

During a conversation itself it is not always easy to pick up on elements that, with retrospect, you should have done. The report gives you the opportunity to go over again the ground you have covered and reflect upon why the conversation went in a certain direction, and why you did not pursue avenues that subsequently seem more important.

- Soon after the conversation, you need to write as closely as possible what you remember was said.

It is usually surprising how much is remembered. A verbatim report is not the equivalent of a tape recording. It is your memory of the conversation, and what you cannot remember may well be as significant as what you can recall. In writing the report you should indicate periods in the sequence which you have forgotten.

- Don't try to write up the whole of a conversation.

You should take a particular bit of the conversation which you find interesting or intriguing, or seems to be a recurrent pattern of behaviour that you want to focus upon.

- Situate the part you are writing in a larger context that can be described in summary, with the verbatim report as a record of the relevant part in sequence.
- For ease of reading, it helps to indicate who is talking by their initial, and number successive contributions made to the conversation.
- Leave a margin on the right hand side of the paper for others, or you, to comment on another occasion.

Reading a verbatim report

When considering a verbatim account in supervision, you might want to take the following points to start the exploration:

- Using the clinical rhombus: who best fits the four points of reflective practitioner, the supervisor, the agency, the 'situation'?
- Using the rhombus: where are the cracks or splits? What are

the pressures? What are the wider socio-political dynamics that need to be considered? What are the power dynamics?

- What voices, present or absent, can you identify? Are there other participants in the account or story? How might each of them hear the conversation?
- Using role play, imagined alter egos (who perhaps attend to feelings or what is not being said by any particular character), group sculpture which is subsequently discussed (where a group are asked to position themselves in silence to express the encounter that the verbatim captures).
- What might have been said or done differently at each point?
- What theological reflection can arise from this report? As a way of provoking theological reflection, questions can be asked about the presence and perspective of God in the situation.
- Attend to the feelings stirred in the group or supervisor as further material for analysis.

The verbatim report opens up interesting possibilities of different interpretation as the text with all its complex interplay is analysed. In practice, as the text is explored with a mentor or in a small group, opportunities to experiment with different courses of action emerge within a safe learning space. The best supervision is that which brings out the dialogical nature of what occurs – the different voices and perspectives so that any given situation can be explored as a rich encounter.

We look now at two verbatim reports provided by Robert and Sarah.

Sarah

I went to get my tyres checked at a local supplier. The mechanic Bob was looking for my toolkit and opened my boot which is stacked high with evangelism resources. He turned and grinned at me and asked,

B1   Are you leaving home?

We both laughed

S1   This is all my work stuff.

B2   Well. What kind of a vicar are you?

S2   I'm an evangelist. I work part time in a church, the rest of the time I travel around the country encouraging people to share their faith with others. I want to connect faith with modern culture and talk about God in a way that makes sense in everyday life. Tapping into people's experiences just like Jesus used to do.

B3   Has anyone ever talked to you about Out of Body Experiences?

S3   No they haven't, but I've heard about these things and I'm open to believe that strange phenomena do happen. Has something like that ever happened to you?

B4   Yes – it's happened a few times. I can see myself from above. The first time it happened during an operation. But then it happened again at home. I lived with a girl for a while and she woke up to find me unable to communicate with her. She researched it and bought me a book on OBE and I tried out one of the exercises but it frightened me so I've never done it since. We're not together now.

S4   Are you saying that you found that the 'essence which is you' – whatever you choose to call it – was able to exist separately from the shell which is your body?

B5   Yes, definitely.

S5   Let me ask you a question then. If that's true, then can you imagine that when your body dies the 'essence which is you' will be able to continue to exist separately?

B6   I've not thought that far ahead but yes, I can see what you mean and I can accept that.

S6   Where would you want it to live?

B7   WOW – that's a powerful question. Are you asking

me to decide whether I want to live in Heaven or Hawaii?

S7   Something like that.

B8   I'll need to think about that one.

S8   Yes, you probably will. But can I just throw some extra things in for you to think about? I believe that God built us and 'wired us up' to be the people we are. He knows every detail of our lives. Only God is able to heal your brokenness and made you whole and happy. Only God knows you intimately and loves you unconditionally. No other person can offer us that.

His eyes were suddenly full of tears and I needed to defuse it for him.

S9   The Bible tells us that God knows how many hairs are on our heads.

I looked at his shaved head.

S10   Mind you – that's not so difficult with you is it?

We both laughed.

He suddenly felt the need to make an urgent phone call.
I left and he waved me off. I've left him to think about it. My customer details are on the computer and we've chatted about my church so he knows where to find me in an emergency. Otherwise I'm leaving it to God to prompt him to follow up the conversation next time I get my tyre treads checked. For the first time in my life I'm praying for a puncture!!!!

Problem is: I feel a bit inadequate about talking about the actual phenomena. I've tapped in OBE on the Internet and there are loads of sites but I wouldn't know which were genuine.

Maybe I don't need to go deeply into it – I might have said enough to make him chat with me on a different level. But it makes me realize that I claim that we serve the Ultimate Supernatural being – but we don't really explore it during training.

Perhaps I should stop reading *Christian Herald* and take up the *New Scientist* instead – this is a serious consideration.

Brought to supervision, for example in a group of peers at theological college or on a course, or as part of a continuing ministerial education (CME) group, the group could be encouraged by its facilitator to consider how Sarah carried forward this conversation, following the initial comments by Bob and how she rounded it off in humour. Her different interventions could be explored and alternatives suggested at various points. Perspectives arising from more or less evangelical standpoints would probably emerge within the group, prompting further discussion about outreach and evangelistic approaches. Subsequently, Sarah emailed me with these further comments about how she reflected upon what she had said, and her comments here could be explored within supervision:

> I did wonder if I'd bombed him a bit – I don't usually go for the jugular in such a direct way. But it tumbled out in a sort of impassioned way. It certainly had an effect.
> Possibly I might have asked more questions and just dropped a tantalizer in – that would be my usual approach. Don't want to put him off asking me anything again . . .
> Anyway – it's few and far between visits. There's always a possibility that people change jobs and a softly, softly approach isn't possible.
> Or they die before you get around to telling them . . .
> I prayed hard though – for quite a while after – that God would repair any damage I might have done.

A supervisor might encourage the group to identify different voices that are present and absent within the conversation, alongside Sarah and Bob. Bob's mention of the 'girl' who introduced him to out of body experiences: she could be identified as another voice. In Bob's mind is Sarah another woman who is introducing him to scary ideas from which he needs to run?

Other more theological questions might arise within the group: What do other members think about OBE? What understandings of the relationship between body and soul do members have? Is the soul 'an essence' and the body 'a shell' as assumed here? Where might they go for more theological study on the subject? How might Sarah take forward her interest in the relation between science and religion?

> If you were Sarah's supervisor, how would you help her to respond to her anxiety that she might have 'done damage' in the situation?
>
> What questions would you ask that could help her to reflect upon the way she handled the conversation with Bob?
>
> What other issues does the conversation and Sarah's subsequent comments raise that you would want to explore?

The facilitator of the group could then write up a verbatim report of the group meeting to take in turn to his own supervision, perhaps in discussion with other tutors. To do so, of course, would require Sarah's permission, or names disguised sufficiently for her not to be recognizable within potentially close organizational circles.

We turn to another verbatim report, provided by Robert. As you read through, imagine you are Robert's supervisor, and he has brought this to you during a supervision session. How would you explore what he has written with him?

Robert

Scene: my first ever funeral visit, literally couldn't see the other end of the room because of cannabis smoke!!! About 7 or 8 family members crammed into the room for the death of their father, who'd been married 3 times to the same lady

. . . I'm afraid I can't distinguish between which family member said what.

R1.   (*On the doorstep of their house*) Morning, my name's Robert, I'm the curate, one of the 'vicars' from Christchurch.

A1.   (*As I'm being shown into the front room*) Hope you're not going to give us a long service, Peter didn't like Church much, a Christian, but not one for Church . . . so you'll keep it short.

R2.   I'll do the best I can, but to do your father justice means I wouldn't want to rush the service.

A2.   (*Really nervous*) There's not much to say about Peter . . . liked a pint, karaoke, women . . . but a real family man, loved by everyone at the Labour club.

About 40 minutes of me taking notes on the details of Peter's life to be able to give a decent homily, then . . .

A3.   We don't want any mention of God in the service, 'cos there doesn't seem much point, he doesn't exist and Peter wasn't into that sort of thing . . . so no prayers, hymns or shit like that . . .

R3.   (*who's currently wishing he'd never been ordained*) To be 100% honest with you, cards on the table . . . I'm a Christian minister, my whole life and job are based upon God and I couldn't in all honesty give you a Christian service without talking about God . . . I don't think it would be fair to me, or actually to you . . . I think God has a lot to do and say with Peter and this funeral service . . . I think it's really important that we talk about God, but if you feel really strongly about this we could arrange for a humanist to come and speak to you . . .

Long silence

R4.   I am genuinely not wanting to make life difficult,

throw God in your face, but I want to offer you the best that I can, and the best support that I can . . . and I believe that involves talking about God . . .

A4.   We're not really that bothered, you can do what you like, it doesn't matter anyway, we've said our good-byes . . .

R5.   Perhaps I could show you what is in the service and we could talk about what you'd like left out, or maybe included . . .

A5.   Can't be bothered with that . . . although Peter did use to like that hymn . . . what it was it again? Sounded like . . . (*unrecognizable humming*)

R6.   If you want to ask the funeral directors they might know it, I don't, sorry . . . the funeral directors have a list of hundreds of favourite hymns; they may have one suitable.

A6.   OK . . . thanks . . . I think that's all we can tell you . . .

R7.   (*at this stage extremely nervous*)
This is going to sound strange, and please feel free to say no, but I like to offer to say a short prayer for people I get to visit . . . would you mind if I said a prayer for you and the family?

A7.   That sounds nice . . .

(silence, literally immediately all bow heads!)

R8.   (*Can't remember the prayer*)

Funeral ended up being huge, nearly 300, and I got loads of thank you cards!!???

What questions would you, as supervisor, ask to begin to explore this funeral visit with Robert and to draw out learning about ministerial practice from it?

What do you think are the main issues for him?

How is power and authority embedded and negotiated within this conversation?

How might the nervousness that Robert identifies in himself and in the family be understood?

Using the points of the clinical rhombus, who might you include at the 'agency' point

• within the situation of the funeral visit?
• in the context of your supervision of him?

In conclusion, verbatim reports can be understood as living human documents that bring to supervision the practice of ministry for further reflection. Clinical Pastoral Education advocates the use of the verbatim account as its main method because they enable the practitioner to examine as closely as possible the actuality of a particular event. Learning from situations such as these, where Sarah and Robert are wanting to explore how they relay their faith, and where they reveal a preparedness to be vulnerable and a willingness to examine situations that had left them with questions, can be extremely valuable both in terms of the self-awareness that they develop and as they explore the theological reflections that arise. Good supervision with a trusted supervisor or a group enables exploration and self-knowledge to grow, and theological insights to be disclosed by reflection upon practice.

5

LEARNING TO WRITE: THE LIVING HUMAN DOCUMENT

Introduction

In the last two chapters the 'space' of supervision has been mapped, using Winnicott's idea of the facilitating environment, and then looking at the interplay of difference by drawing on Taylor's and Volf's work. We have also looked at how the space of supervision requires clear boundaries so that different dynamics and aspects of reflection upon ministerial practice can be explored with skilled listening. Those working within Clinical Pastoral Education tend to use verbatim reports; but a case study, a journal entry, or a video recording, relevant letters, autobiography, creative writing could also be used. We saw in the last chapter how the material will contain dialogue, and as it is brought for reflection it provokes other dialogues, implicit in the initial encounter but then enriched as the supervisor or group explore further. The verbatim account becomes a 'living human document' as it comes alive in the hands of supervisor and reflective practitioner or a group.

Up to now we have primarily been considering the 'space' of supervision: what makes it a safe place so that challenging material can be considered and potentially difficult learning can be worked through. In this chapter we shift ground somewhat to explore further the nature of dialogue.

The expression 'living human document' can be understood

in a number of ways. Anton Boisen, the founder of CPE, originally used it to refer to the actual person, but as that person turns a moment of their life into text, it can, I think, be also understood as the text itself that captures life for further reflection. The diary entries of the six ministers are 'living human documents' as they give us a sense of lives turned into text. Jackie's portfolio is a living human document. The verbatim accounts of Sarah and Robert in the last chapter enable them to reflect further on the conversations they had. Such texts can be used in supervision, or – the main content of this chapter – they can become the main method for continuing self-supervision and reflection in the form of a learning journal.

Journals are increasingly used in professional development (Bolton, 2003; Moon, 2004) as a way of enabling reflection upon practice and lifelong learning. In this chapter, we turn from consideration of supervision with others, either one-to-one or in a group, to keeping a journal. It may be thought that a journal is essentially a private activity, but here the journal will be seen as a text that is dialogical in the ways it reflects life and the practice of ministry. At the heart of a journal is conversation, oneself to another, as Ricoeur terms it (1994), and it can be expressed in different forms of writing – letters, poems, email messages, sermons, critical self-appraisals, doodles, all of which can be pasted in as material for ongoing self-supervision.

A Turn to the Self

This chapter, then, represents a deliberate turn to the self, but not in order to foster a solipsistic or narcissistic view of identity. Identity is understood here as always in dialogue with others, and with itself, in concrete situations. To study the self as and through a living human document is to focus upon one's own behaviour, patterns of non-verbal forms of communication and attitudes so that personal and professional growth can occur in response to the challenge of the difference of others. The word 'reflexivity' is often understood as a turn to the dialogical self so that awareness may develop of one's cultural embeddedness in social and political dynamics, to focus on communication and action by externalizing 'the self'.

In *Modernity and Identity*, Giddens argues that self-reflexivity is a necessary aspect of late modern identity, as individuals and institutions turn their ways of knowing and analysing on themselves, continually assessing and hypothesizing on actions and practice. In a post-traditional era, he writes, identity is no longer dependent upon one's place in the order of things. A reflexive turn to the self becomes an inevitable aspect of the modern structure of knowledge (1991/2003, pp. 20–21). It could be argued (as Flyvjberg, 2001, has done) that it was a way of knowing that was implicit as Aristotle developed his concept of practical wisdom or phronesis. This has always required a reflexive ability, the ability to analyse one's own actions and behaviour. Whether this is the case or not, Giddens is certainly right, that the modern era has seen an intensification of that turn to the self, the development of reflexivity.

Reflexivity / Reflection

What of the difference between reflection and reflexivity? Do these two words mean the same? Bolton makes an explicit distinction between being reflective and reflexive:

> The practitioner has to be reflexive as well as reflective. Being *reflexive* is focusing close attention upon *one's own* actions, thoughts and feelings and their effects; being *reflective* is looking at the *whole scenario*: other people, the situation and place, and so on. (2003, p. 7, her emphasis)

Bolton focuses in this way on the two aspects of reflection/ reflexivity, but does not set up a dualism between the two. She argues that there is a true interplay between attention to the inner self and the outer focus on the context. For example, you cannot know yourself except as you act in the world, relating with others, finding yourself in certain situations. You cannot reflect on your actions without thinking about how you usually respond, without some self-knowledge. The two are intimately connected. It is the same person who reflects in both aspects – only when you are being 'reflexive', you turn your gaze on yourself; when you are being reflective you are examining how you acted in some situation or another. Any action in the world will be profoundly affected by certain factors that need reflexive attention. For example, how I am in an interfaith situation will depend largely on how aware I am of transcultural issues, how able I am to see the world through perspectives other than the one I consciously and unconsciously consider 'normal'. The reflexive work I do, giving attention to my own attitudes and prejudices, will greatly affect my grasp of the complexities of relations of power between people of differ- ence. The extent to which, in reflexive exploration, I grow in openness to the perspectives and outlook of someone who lives with a disability, for instance, or someone of a different class or sexual identity to my own, will influence how I engage in that context and with that person.

The reflection on any particular encounter, then, becomes a reflexive activity as I examine what I thought and said. I become changed as I take up the reflective and reflexive opportunities that supervision offers. This can be done within the pages of a journal as time and space is given to further reflection. Bolton writes that 'a reflective, educational process does not allow anything to be taken for granted. We need to walk away from things in order for them to come into focus. Why?, how?, what?, who?, where?, when?, need to be asked of everything – all the time' (2003, pp. 34–5).

The Dialogical Self

The living human document, the life-turned-into-text, which is reflective of practice and reflexive of self, is embedded in dialogue, with words and thoughts going between self and others in an ongoing conversation which is both internal and external. To understand identity in this way is to draw upon dialogical theory. Dialogical theory really began with the work of Mikhail Bakhtin. Bakhtin (1895–1975) was a literary theorist who lived and worked in Russia after the Revolution. Years of intense creativity in collaboration with his two friends Medvedev and Voloshinov become increasingly dangerous after Stalin began to consolidate his power in the 1920s. Bakhtin was arrested in 1929 and spent six years in exile in Soviet Central Asia. Voloshinov died of TB in 1936; Medvedev was shot in 1938. Bakhtin has been seen as a writer who kept a sense of freedom alive through Stalin's terror. His writing on carnival, seemingly innocent to the authorities, carried a subversive sub-text that challenged totalitarian power. His writing on the ways in which texts, and particularly novelistic texts, bear various different voices (heteroglossia), and his exploration of dialogical, as opposed to monological, literary forms has opened up many fruitful lines of thought through the twentieth and twenty-first centuries in his influence on many later philosophers and literary theorists.

In one of his essays in *The Dialogic Imagination* (1996), entitled 'Epic and Novel', he writes about the epic form and its main character, the hero:

As such he is a fully finished and completed being. This has been accomplished on a lofty heroic level, but what is complete is something hopelessly ready-made; he is all there, from beginning to end he coincides with himself, he is absolutely equal to himself . . . He has already become everything he could become, and he could become only that which he has already become. He is entirely externalized in

the most elementary, almost literal sense: everything in him
is exposed and loudly expressed. (p. 34)

In his description of such a figure – a literary type, to be sure
– you can hear, I think, Bakhtin commenting on a totalitarian
mindset: the Stalinist bureaucrat dehumanized by his function-
ality so that no longer was there any play between internal and
external, no dynamic growth or sense of development. There
is no nuance of appearance or action, no subtlety of voice
or layer of meaning. It is a characterization. It is an extreme
description. But I use it because I think it is possible to detect
traces of this heroic type, sometimes, when the word 'formation' is used, and in particular understandings of ministry that
rely upon a clericalized paradigm.

By way of contrast to the static and received form of the
hero of the epic, Bakhtin opens up the novel as a text in which
a variety of voices is to be heard:

> The novel orchestrates all its themes, the totality of the
> world of objects and ideas depicted and expressed in it,
> by means of the social diversity of speech types and by the
> differing individual voices that flourish under such condi-
> tions. Authorial speech, the speeches of narrators, inserted
> genres, the speech of characters are merely those fundamen-
> tal compositional unities with whose help heteroglossia can
> enter the novel; each of them permits a multiplicity of social
> voices and a wide variety of their links and interrelationships
> (always more or less dialogized). These distinctive links and
> interrelationships between utterances and languages, this
> movement of the theme through different languages and
> speech types, its dispersion into the rivulets and droplets
> of social heteroglossia, its dialogization – this is the basic
> distinguishing feature of the stylistics of the novel. (p. 263)

Again, you can read into this text Bakhtin's subversion of the
monoculture of Stalinism. Here he celebrates the diversity
of voice and the complexity of interaction between different

characters, including the author, which can be found within
a novel. Life itself, you might say, is to be discovered in all its
multiplicity of dialogue and speech, in its diversity, its social
heteroglossia.

Incomplete, unfinished, a dialogical self is constructed as one
amongst many voices, in constant negotiation. Lynne Pearce
says that 'the Bakhtinian subject . . . is formed and re-formed
through a never-ending process of sociolinguistic interaction'
(1994, p. 89). Formation, when understood in these terms as
a constant forming and re-forming, loses that connotation of
static completeness, that sense of arrival. Instead it is possible
to see the self as in a continuous process where the encounter with many others in ongoing conversations shapes us and
reshapes us, transforming and changing the way we are, who
we are. So instead of taking a stance and making pronounce-
ments, as Bakhtin would see it, in a monological way, we need
to be there, in the thick of the dialogue, contributing ourselves
and what we think, but always open to what others are saying
and thinking, always open to be changed. There is provision-
ality about this dialogic sense of self, which encourages the
ability to be creative with possibilities rather than reliant upon
certainties.

So where does dialogue take place within ministry? Most
obviously in the encounters with work colleagues, members of
the congregation, others in the local community, as the minister collaborates on a project, or negotiates a shared vision for
the future. As Robert visited Peter's family, as Sarah talked
with Bob. But the dialogue is also an internal one. Consider
the significant others with whom you converse in your mind
as you walk the children to school. As you wonder what your
mother or father would say to a particular course of action
you are thinking about. What comment a soul friend, or
mentor, or spiritual director might make. And as we fall into
the hands of the living God, we dialogue in prayer, in listening to biblical texts for the voice of God; we are engaged in
dialogue which transforms us. Sarah, in her subsequent email
to me, indicated something of the internal dialogues she had

been having, including prayer. Internally she was playing with and considering different possibilities, different ways in which she might have responded in that situation. We form practical judgements; we use practical wisdom, phronesis, which is shaped in conversation, external and internal. When I first started exploring whether ordination was the right path for me, I spoke with my parish priest at the time, and over subsequent years built up a good friendship with him. He died over ten years ago now, but I still find myself in conversation with him, imagining what he would say, taking on board and being changed, even now, by his influence. And as John V. Taylor would say, the go-between God is present in such encounters, enabling that conversation, whether external, with real people, or internal – imagined, but nonetheless a powerful dialogue – that forms and transforms our sense of self.

Dialogue: Difference and Power

Such dialogues, especially the external ones, need to be understood as always belonging to specific times and places and permeated through with different registers of difference. Our conversations – how and what we say – are dependent upon the context and the people with whom we are speaking. We talk differently to a child, to our boss, to a friend, to someone of another faith and culture, and our conversations are always pervaded by explicit or implicit relations of power. Robert, as he shared his faith with Peter's family who were reluctant to let any mention of God be made at the funeral, was nervous because he felt he had to share his faith and feared they would reject something important to him. He took the risk that he might be interpreted as imposing his faith on others. The conversation was power-laden in complex ways. Robert Stam has written:

> To speak of dialogue, without speaking of power, in a Bakhtinian perspective is to speak meaninglessly, in a void.

For Bakhtin, language is thus everywhere imbricated with asymmetries of power. Patriarchal domination and economic dependency make sincere interlocution impossible. There is no 'neutral' utterance; language is everywhere shot through with intentions and accents; it is material, multiaccentual, and historical, and is densely overlaid with the traces of its historical usages. (1989, p. 8)

Stam refers here to patriarchal power and economic dependency. He argues that to be in a dynamic where one is economically dependent or subordinated in a dominant patriarchal culture mars the conditions of free speech – can even destroy them. It is not that interlocution cannot happen at all; it just will not be 'sincere' if the imbalance of power between those conversing is too great.

Stam says that no utterance is ever 'neutral' – it will always carry with it some negotiation with or from a position of dominance and subordination. As we consider what enables effective reflective practice, it is important that we attend reflexively to our own position in terms of the power relations we have with those we dialogue with.

How do you understand power to be present in the funeral visit that Robert made with Peter's family?

Consider a situation when you have felt constrained or silenced by differentials of power. How did you feel? What did you do?

Those who have used Bakhtin's ideas have argued that all dialogue is permeated by power relations, and an important aspect of reflexivity in ministry is the appreciation of one's own positionality and power in any encounter: that we are part of a conversation that is a constant negotiation with others, with the self, and with God. Relations of power permeate all dialogue. Stam says here that dialogue is material. It is not as if voices float around in the ether, but that every dialogue, every

conversation takes place in a real situation, in a real context
between real bodies, between embodied self and embodied
other. To be engaged in dialogue with sensitivity, one needs
to be aware of the complex ways in which we communicate
with others.

A Dialogical, Embodied Self

The way in which self negotiates with others has become an
increasingly important aspect of twentieth- and twenty-first-
century thought. Emmanuel Levinas wrote in the aftermath
of the Holocaust about the necessity of encounter with 'the
other'. He was born in 1906 into an orthodox Jewish family
in Lithuania, and as Martin Buber enquires into the 'I and
Thou', Levinas examined the relationship between the self
and other, but brought a different emphasis to the encounter
by focusing upon the face, the most obvious material point
of contact. Levinas, after the experience of Nazism and the
Holocaust, argued that the other could not be understood,
as Buber had done, as 'friendly'; rather the face of the other
questioned the self, challenged the self with its misery. There
was no necessary communication between self and other, but
rather dia / logue, marked by rupture. From his experiences
he could envisage a gulf of non-communication. He attended
to what was silenced in any encounter, to that which is 'not
said'. Instead of the subject, the knowing I who relates as an
autonomous self with its others, Levinas thought of the self as
first and foremost a 'me', placed in the accusative, accused by
its others, responsible to its others. In the relationship with the
other, the self is challenged, 'wrench[ing] from ourselves the
autonomy of our consciousness and intentions, by the demand
of the other and the responsibility this lays (and has always
laid) upon us' (Ward, 2000, p. 101). The other is found in the
face, in the encounter that can be a terrible non-encounter.
Behind that (non-) encounter is otherness that is radically different, wholly other, and which cannot be captured in words.

Levinas distinguished between the said, which is done with, completed, and the infinite, the unsaid, the unthinkable which leaves its trace in what is said, and perhaps here Levinas could be seen to refer to God. As Ward writes:

> The infinite (and God) enters Levinas' work because the saying which arrives with the face of the other person bears witness to an elsewhere, a transcendence which is totally other . . . Here we move beyond being . . . towards that which is otherwise than being. This is the Good beyond being . . . [and] it is from this transcendental Good that the command, the saying, the call to and of responsibility issues. (2000, p. 102)

In this call is located desire: Levinas marks human being and existence with desire. It is the sense of being divided, incomplete, that draws us on in desire: 'we are both commanded by, and attracted to, the other which draws us ever beyond – beyond ourselves, beyond the given, beyond history, beyond Being itself. We submit as servants, as suffering servants, both to the command and the attraction' (2000, p. 104). So here, in contrast to the theology of the presence of the Holy Spirit as the go-between God, going between self and other, we have a sense of God who is beyond language, beyond dialogue, the object of desire, and the subject to whom we respond as object, a subject who calls us ever beyond, encountered as the Other in the others with whom we dialogue.

Levinas enables us to see how a sense of self can be formed and transformed in dialogue with others, and in response to the Other, who draws us on into the future by the very difference and strangeness which is hinted to us in the face of the people with whom we dialogue, provoking our desire for what we are not. As Heather Walton has commented, 'the self is constituted through a mysterious meeting with what lies beyond its bounds' (2000, p. 12).

So if self is seen as always dialogical, and pulled towards the future in desire for the ultimate Other, then 'formation' is never complete. We ourselves need to view ourselves as

partial, incomplete, open to encounter, open to transformation by the difference of the other, with whom dialogue may,
at times, be extremely difficult, marked by rupture.

Think about a time when you have been in dialogue with
another and have been aware that the cultural assumptions that lie beneath your conversation are very different, even incommensurable. Describe or draw how it
felt.
    How might Taylor's writing of the go-between God
taken you forward?

If Levinas wrote about how the face relays the encounter
with others, then, by extension, bodies too can be seen to
convey meaning. How they are used, dressed, presented are
important elements in communication. Many of these same
issues of dialogue and communication between self and other
are inscribed in ethnography, the discipline of researching and
writing about culture. Ethnographers seek cultures to study
that are not necessarily to be found on far distant shores:
many today will look at a local congregation, or a school and
its subcultures, as 'fields' of research. The local, close to home,
the familiar can provide as much interest as the very strange.
Amanda Coffey carried out an ethnographic study on a firm of
accountants, and noted how dress functioned to communicate
certain values:

The physical appearance of accountants is of course
important. Certainly to an outsider the accountant is perceived as fulfilling certain expectations about dress and
demeanour. In Western Ridge, the firm in which I conducted
fieldwork, new recruits (in this case graduate accountants)
were given implicit and explicit guidance on their personal
appearance. This included not only dress but also advice
on skin care, makeup, hair-style, body hair, and the use
of props such as jewellery and briefcases. For these junior
accountants the body was implicated in their daily work

lives. By association it was also implicated in my personal and practical experiences of fieldwork. (1999, p. 66)

As she researched, Coffey found that she herself had changed her own appearance, unconsciously, in order to engage in the 'field' as effectively as possible:

> During my fieldwork I was not particularly self-conscious or reflexive about the production of my own body: certainly not beyond the realities of needing to look the part in order to achieve access and an acceptable fieldwork persona. In retrospect I have come to realize that I was engaged in negotiating and producing a fieldwork body. In doing so I was responding to norms and rules of the organization. I crafted my body as part of the crafting of the field, and this was not something that was confined to the actual fieldwork setting. The ways I 'chose' to dress, wear make-up, style my hair, even shave my legs were part of a bodily performance which I subconsciously thought necessary for the successful accomplishment of the fieldwork. My body is part of the way in which I experienced fieldwork and an important aspect of my fieldwork memories. I will always remember the ways in which the graduate accountants sought to craft the image of accountant. As too I will remember the way in which my feet ached after a working day in high-heeled shoes! (p. 66)

A Dialogical, Embodied, Public Self

From the dialogue of voice, to the otherness of face, to the crafting of body. The (trans)formation of self calls for a constant negotiation with the otherness of the field or context, which includes the personal and emotional. Much of what Coffey writes for ethnographers applies equally well to ministers, who use, perhaps unknowingly, ethnographic methods of participant observation as they engage in local contexts and seek to understand the culture of a congregation or local organizations. As Coffey 'crafts' her body, so many ministers think carefully about what to wear for a funeral visit, or for a primary school assembly, or to lead both in one morning. What signals are given? Not always, today, a message of safety and reliability, but now often inviting the label of authoritarian, or patriarchal, or too traditional to understand the contemporary world, sometimes even incurring taunts and despising comment, or distrust. In different contexts of ministry, when working on a project, or with secular organizations, a self-reflexive minister will recognize the importance of developing such social and communication skills, attending to what is said and not said and how the body speaks.

How much consideration do you give to the way you present your body? What do you communicate, do you think, to others by the way you habitually dress?

To understand oneself as an embodied dialogical self will prompt consideration of the personal vulnerability, even risk, which can result from public ministry. The situations that call for caution will be different for men and for women, for able-bodied or ministers with physical difficulties. If you are black, or belong to an ethnic minority, then your awareness of threat in different situations will probably be enhanced. The negotiation of relations of power becomes an important aspect of the experience of ministry if you enter any given context knowing from past encounters that you may be on the receiving end of the prejudices of others. Levinas' ethical understanding of the self as subject to the other takes on a different depth of meaning when the self is someone who is used to working as a non-dominant person. Reflexivity and self-awareness will tend to be understood differently depending on the experience of the minister, and what the minister and any other person he or she encounters has internalized from the past in terms of the differentials of power around, for instance, age and generational issues, class, gender, ethnicity, faith, sexuality. A minister who is able to be reflexive will be aware to a greater or lesser extent of dominating in any situation.

The Negotiation of Intimacy

The practice of ministry often brings encounters of an intimate nature with individuals and families, and dialogue as embodied communication includes the negotiation of intimacy. Self-reflexivity calls for reflection upon areas such as sexual attraction, touch, the communication of closeness. Coffey writes here as an ethnographer, but her words resonate too with the experience of ministry:

> Establishing and managing intimacy and distance is a bodily skill. We 'learn' the craft skills of body work during fieldwork participation. We get to know when it is appropriate or acceptable to touch bodies – whether that be affectionate slaps on the back, hugs, shaking hands, physical proximity or kissing. Moreover we learn when it is unacceptable to engage in body contact – where the body is distinct and bounded. Violating body rules can jeopardize the role of the researcher and the quality of field relations. (1999, p. 73)

Write about a time when you got it wrong . . . where you misjudged the appropriateness of touch. How could you tell? How did you find out?

A public minister needs, as a reflexive self, to consider the ways in which sexual activity, desire and expectation impact upon their ministry. As a dialogical and embodied person he or she will inevitably have a sexual positionality which requires alert awareness of what is an appropriate level of engagement, and what is inappropriate, to avoid transgressing professional guidelines of conduct. Sometimes we find ourselves repeating patterns of behaviour and response that we learned long ago, which can become a natural reaction to a similar situation in the present. A colleague told me how she used to fancy Ben, a friend of her brother. When a new Roman Catholic priest joined her clergy fellowship group, he was Ben's spitting image. She found herself beginning to relate to the priest in ways that belonged to that former relationship. She had transferred her feelings from the one situation to this one, and was able to catch herself doing it.

How much are we prepared to share with others? What do we keep hidden? How far are we prepared to trust? Are we confident that what we share will be held safely? Important questions, these. Much we hide from others, and much can be hidden to ourselves, and we often need others to help us by reflecting back what we cannot see. The strength of a good critical friend, either in supervision, mentoring, consultancy or spiritual direction is that that person is able to hear us within a situation of trust, where we are held sufficiently to be creative and explore other possibilities as we continue to change and respond to the call of God. And when we fall into the hands of the living God, spending time with the God to whom all hearts are open, all desires known, we can, in prayer, reflect upon ourselves, retreating in order perhaps to assimilate justified criticism with a sense of humility, or perhaps develop the confidence to return to something that needs further exploration and understanding.

The Learning Journal

A journal can provide the space to explore ourselves, to have conversation with ourselves as we grow to understand our motivations, desires and actions in more profound ways. To do so enables the reflective practitioner, at the heart of a complex web of interdependent relationships, to engage more effectively in ministry and life. So, after exploring at some length and depth the nature of dialogue and reflexivity, we turn now to how writing can serve as a method of reflection.

Bolton writes about how a reflective practitioner can use the processes of writing. She comments that practitioners do not think and then write, but the writing itself is the vehicle for the reflection as the processes of reading drafts, interacting and responding to what has been written, means the initial writing is interpreted, clarifying and extending the writer's thinking and understanding (2003, chapter 9).

Geoff returned to his living human document a year after he initially wrote.

Looking back after the space of a year at my account of three days, I was surprised that I did not mention what I find is the constant component of my ministry. For me action is always and quite naturally accompanied by reflection. By that I mean much more than an instantaneous reaction to what is going. Reflection is at least the following – thinking, praying (alone or with others), being in dialogue with scripture and tradition, and having conversations with other people. All this is for me a constant backdrop to the activity of ministry and it is how I learn as I live and work, so as to move forward, to change and to help others to change as well.

Since I wrote my account our team ministry seems to be developing new ways of working and learning together. I described a meeting at which the Team Council had begun to engage with the reality of one parish's situation. That seems to have helped us to find our way towards working together at a different and deeper level of dialogue and involvement with each other. I had always been wary of imposing an agenda or a strategy on the Team Council, believing that it would eventually find its role through engaging with the issues as they appeared before us. It has seemed to take a long time for the Council to make a difference or for people in the parishes to see the point of the team, in spite of some very successful shared events. Now it is becoming more of a real focus for shared thinking and action.

Here Geoff reflects upon how he reflects, using the team

ministry as a way of working through the issues and concerns that face his churches. He writes how 'Reflection is at least the following – thinking, praying (alone or with others), being in dialogue with scripture and tradition, and having conversations with other people. All this is for me a constant backdrop to the activity of ministry and it is how I learn as I live and work, so as to move forward, to change and to help others to change as well.' He describes a lifelong habit of reflection upon practice. His writing down and reviewing enabled him to enter into dialogue with himself, clarifiying what he had initially left out, giving him an opportunity to examine positions which perhaps had not previously been thought through.

Such processes of writing and reviewing, redrafting and interpreting are to be found in the practice of journal-writing, in an ongoing, disciplined way. A journal allows reflection upon experience and practice by turning lived experiences and relationships into a written account, a text, a living human document. This document becomes an external account which can then be available for consideration and further analysis and examination. It can offer the opportunity for theological reflection upon new experiences as God is encountered and encounters us in life and ministry.

Jennifer Moon describes this process of learning from writing and reviewing: 'When we ask learners to write about an event only once, there is a loss of the richness of the real experience of reflection in which we turn events around and see them differently over a period of time' (2004, p. 169). She says that redrafting and reviewing written work enables the 'useful outcome . . . to cause the learner to shift from one frame of reference to others – to recognize that there are "two sides" to most arguments' (p. 171). She advocates the use of dialogue techniques whereby the writer introduces the issue under consideration in a short paragraph and then prompts dialogue, 'listening' to the imagined voice of the other, writing the words, then responding, and so on: 'dialogues can travel over remarkable and unexpected territory and yield useful learning' (p. 171).

The living human document as a journal becomes a narrative, a story that twists and turns, that breaks and ruptures, that has continuity in the past, but tells a story with an open future. Writing is a crucial element in this process. Time to write offers the opportunity to express ourselves, to reflect and learn. Writing in this way helps us to be reflexive, to be open to change – and as such it can foster personal and professional growth. Bolton notes the creative aspects of writing, how stories and poetry offer explorative material (2003, p. 5), and effective reflective practice is the focusing upon detailed stories of practice and life, and upon the thoughts and feelings associated with the actions in them. These stories are imaginative creations drawn from experience (p. 7) and can hold the ambiguities and losses of life. They can enable us to make meaning of failures, enable us to live with gaps and frustrations.

So what sort of document or text might we be talking about that can convey this sense of identity that is ourselves in the world of today? All sorts of styles of writing can be included: any relevant letter, email, newspaper article, creative writing and verbatim account. Bolton says that the processes of writing are essentially playful, just as any sort of creativity is playful. One of the exercises she offers is this (p. 120):

Choose a comfortable uninterrupted place and time, and writing materials you like.

Make sure you have everything else you need to hand – like coffee and chocolate biscuits.

Be able to time yourself to write without stopping for about six minutes.

Allow another 30–40 minutes or so after the six, in order to do the next bit.

Without stopping to think too hard about it, jot down right now:

Your feelings about undertaking a piece of writing.

Your thoughts on the advantages and disadvantages of writing reflectively.

A journal can take any form: there are many different ways to write a journal, a living human document that reflects the life of the writer. It does help, however, to write regularly, daily, or every two or three days, otherwise you can lose track, or you start to write because you feel you must. Bolton argues that 'the learning journal is the cornerstone of reflective practice work' (p. 159). It can include a myriad of invaluable reflective material: 'free flow *six minute* type writing, stories, poems, musings or reflections upon an event, dialogues with the self, fictional dialogues or monologues with others such as patients, clients or students, analysis of motives and actions, philosophising on such as ethics, evaluation, assessment of practice, description, fantasy used to aid insight, cathartic writing, letters, extended metaphors, ethnography' (p. 160). She suggests these questions to guide writing (p. 155):

- What was *done* one any particular occasion
- What was *thought* about it
- What was *felt* about it

To begin with, most people write descriptive material – telling it how it is, or was. Moon says that writing gains depth as it shows reflection upon what is described, and depth comes with the presence in the text of different perspectives, imaginative or otherwise, interwoven in the description. She talks of 'dialogic reflection', which demonstrates a 'stepping back' from the events and actions described, leading to a different level of mulling around discourse with self and exploring the discourse of events and actions. Such reflection recognizes that there are different qualities of judgement and alternative explanations which may exist for the same material. Moon explains that 'critical reflection . . . demonstrates an awareness that actions and events are not only located within and explicable by multiple perspectives, but are located in and influenced by multiple historical and socio-political contexts'. For her, depth of reflective learning implies a development in the ability to use different frames of reference with associated flexibility, openness and awareness (2004, pp. 97–9). As the reflective practitioner goes back to review and then to review again, often commenting on the original text, and over-layering it with subsequent reflection, working at what other perspectives or courses of action might have been or are possible in a given situation, so the journal becomes more and more useful as a reflective tool of self-supervision.

Moon advocates (p. 148) a double entry journal design. She advises learners to write only on one page of a double spread or on one half of a vertically divided page. The blank space is there until another time when they go through the initial material. Then further writing can generate comment that emerges from a more coherent overview of the initial work. In reviewing the journal in this way, the reflective practitioner acts 'as their own critical friend', and the journal becomes a text overlaid and thick with other associations (Bolton, 2003, p. 149). It is important to be as honest and specific as possible, both in the initial writing and in the reviewing. At the reviewing stage, the journal can be brought into dialogue with other texts – the Bible, other theological or spiritual resources. It can become an aid to prayer, as letters to God, as meditative prayers, hymns, poetry.

Osborn (1988) suggests other techniques to use: including techniques like 'a map of your soul country'. One's life can be described, using allegory as John Bunyan did, as a forest of confusion, a cliff of withdrawal, a river with its different tributaries and streams. Or a body map – an outline picture of yourself without your clothes. How do you feel about it? Mark on the map the places about which you feel embarrassment, pain, energy, excitement, expectation, tiredness. Write about how your body expresses yourself through appearance, demeanour, sensuality, physical regimes. Osborn uses the metaphor of a clock and a clock face to explore what time is it in one's life; what more you want to achieve; times which have gone quickly, or slowly; times which have an identifiable span; how you understand mortality.

He offers an 'us and them' list, which he says is
particularly good for uncovering prejudices. On one side
a list of everyone you feel comfortable with (us); on the
other, individuals and groups who make you uncomfortable (them). What good features can you think of for each
of the entries in the 'them' column?

A learning journal can offer a useful method to support lifelong learning. As an educational discipline it is receiving some
attention at the present time, but of course, journals and auto-
biographical writing have a long history. The potential for
honest reflection, humour, playfulness and the exploration of
difficult problems is there.

Writing with Emotion

Moon argues cogently for the recognition of the ways in which
emotion plays a significant part in learning. She uses several
illustrations of the way in which emotion can impede learning,
when someone is lacking in confidence, anxious and fearful,
and we return to this in the next chapter. But emotion can be a
positive aspect of learning, more positive than Moon conveys.
One of the best examples of emotion and learning is found in
Jo Ind's book *Memories of Bliss* (2003), where she describes
herself working in a library at an essay on whether there
was a coherent system of thought in Coleridge's *Biographia
Literaria*.

> When I had first read the *Biographia* I hadn't had a clue
> what it was about . . . and now I was rereading the reread-
> ing and wondering why Coleridge hadn't done this work
> for himself. Surely it was his job to create coherence in his
> work, not mine. But as I read I was building up little pockets
> of understanding . . . but I still couldn't see what all the
> disparate bits had got to do with each other. I was begin-
> ning to despair that I ever would. Suddenly, I had a thought,

or more precisely one part of my mind made an imaginative leap. In that unexpected moment I glimpsed how the *Biographia* made sense as a whole. It was like turning up the ace of spades . . . My one imaginative leap enabled me to see how those disparate pieces were interconnected; what's more I was able to see that that imaginative leap was what Coleridge had been writing about and that was why he had not written the *Biographia* as a straight, logical system. He had created a work which teased out the imagination of the reader instead.

It was an intellectual discovery but I experienced that moment of it all coming together as a physical sensation. I looked around me. The library was the same sterile environment it had always been but I was hot all over. The thoughts were rushing, bringing a flush of adrenalin in their wake. I wanted to carry on thinking but I was experiencing such a burst of energy that I couldn't sit still. I left the library, jumped on my bike and pedalled around the city, writing the essay in my head as I went. The creative whirling of my mind was echoed in the onward, circling of my feet/pedals/wheels. (2003, pp. 20–22)

I quote the passage at length because of the way in which learning is shown to be a physical as well as an intellectual business, an emotionally-charged, exciting – and despairing – process that, as the learning becomes owned, it becomes internalized and integrated, it becomes part of who you are, your identity. Moon sees learning in these terms too, and it is rarely, if ever, achieved at this depth through the banking or 'brick' methods outlined in Chapter 2 above. Real learning involves sophisticated levels (and look how Ind went around and around her texts, in the attempt to understand) of reflection. Writing a journal can provide important safe space that can function like a retreat from the business of life and ministry, a retreat in order to reflect more deeply, and as such, a journal can be a method of theological reflection. Moon points out that 'reflection slows the pace of learning' (2004, p. 88), and offers space in this sort of way.

In this chapter we have explored the nature of dialogue and dialogical identity. We have taken further Boisen's phrase of 'the living human document' as a way of understanding how life can be turned into text, providing material for reflection upon self. Journal-writing has been explored with its potential for ongoing learning and reflection on life and professional development, for when a learning journal is kept, alongside course material, or the practice of work, ministry and life, new knowledge can be generated, and the skills in processes of reflection acquired and honed. We have thought about how the journal can be seen as a living human document that allows us to retreat and return to the practice of ministry and life.

If you have been keeping a learning journal alongside your reading of the book, read over what you have written (or painted) to date. What reflections would you make on your journal as a method to enable you to learn?

As a method of reflective practice, what would/does journal-writing offer to you?

What are its strengths?   What are its weaknesses?

6

LEARNING TO LEARN: GOOD AND BAD RESISTANCE

Learning is not easy. It can stir defences, anxieties, fear of failure and resistance to change. I have tried to present the space of supervision as a place where there is enough safety to enable change to happen and where different perspectives can be engaged with in dialogue. For learning to happen, resistance to learning needs to be taken seriously. In this chapter we explore how emotion plays an important part in the processes of learning. Resistance can also be felt when the 'facilitating environment' is not good enough, for example when issues of power are not addressed.

Learning and Change

John Hull wrote about learning and change, and how it takes place at the core of identity:

Every emergence out of a taken for granted world of meaning is accompanied by emotion. The emergence is an emergency. The motion in terms of which the self evolves is experienced subjectively as e-motion. The experience will, in fact, be of a complex mass or series of various emotions, and within them will always be emotions of distress and anxiety. Depression and even anguish are often experienced as the emotions associated with the early stages of emergence. This takes place when the old me can now be reflected upon by the newly emerging me, which is beginning to be conscious of it. The anxiety, in other words, is over the loss of the self, at a time when it is still too early to describe it as the previous self. It is the grief felt at emerging from the embedded self into something which I do not yet recognize as being me. It is the experience of birth and re-birth. This sense of confusion, doubt, loss of self and anxiety gradually disappears as the consciousness of a new self settles down and a relation is formed between it and the previous self in memory. At this point, there will often be a feeling of repugnance, of anger and repudiation against the former self and this anger is part of the distancing or differentiation which is necessary if the evolution is to proceed to the next step. (1985, p. 178)

Any educational process, if it is to promote greater understanding and real learning in a given situation, will provoke anxiety. Learning is an encounter with something new, something challenging, which requires assimilation into an existing world view. Reflection upon practice, either in the pages of a journal, or in the space offered by supervision, should result in practice which is different to what was exercised before. To change previous patterns of thinking and doing can be an exciting but daunting process, however much experience we have.

In any situation of new learning, anxiety levels will be high. There will be fear of making mistakes, especially in the public aspects of ministry. There will be fears of rejection, sometimes at very personal levels. Robert's nervousness on his funeral visit was largely about the fear of the family rejecting what he stood for, his faith. Other fears can emerge: What about Mr Jones, who really doesn't want me to visit because I'm a female minister? Will I encounter any comments because I'm black? How do I keep it hidden from my colleagues in ministry that I'm gay? Many ministers in the public gaze will carry hidden anxieties that often circulate around a fear of exposure, or a fear of failure, often heightened if they feel a need to perform that much better in order to avoid the perception that being 'different' is somehow second-best.

Similar anxieties may well be in the mind and heart of the supervisor:

- 'This is the first time I've done this.'
- 'I didn't have a good experience of training myself. I'm determined that the student minister will have a good experience, but I'm worried about getting it wrong.'
- 'Should I make friends with her? Or will that impair our working relationship?'
- 'What happens if we don't get on? How will I handle that?'
- 'How do I introduce experience so I get the pacing right, and he's not overwhelmed all at once?'
- 'What sort of reflection are we going to do together?'
- 'How do we evaluate how successful we've been in this learning situation?'
- 'What happens if it all goes pear-shaped?'

Being in a situation of potential new learning has been described by Moon as the expansion of an existing cognitive map by allowing the new knowledge to be absorbed and to make a difference. John Hull turns to Personal Construct Theory (PCT) to describe a similar process (for further reading see Burr and Butt, 2000; Dalton and Dunnet, 2000; Fransella and Dalton, 2000; Fransella, 2003).

Personal Constructs

George Kelly, who developed PCT in 1955, suggested that people construct interpretive frameworks to enable them to make sense of the world and their experience. Knowledge advances through the adoption of new perspectives, new frameworks. With a personal construct in place, a person is guided in their actions by the construction they hold about themselves and the world around them. Kelly believed that if you want to help people to change you must first understand that construction, the theories they hold and the questions they are asking.

A personal construct, a framework that enables meaning to be made of experience, will be used as it proves itself serviceable through life. New experience needs to be integrated within the core structures that make up the personal construct. If the new experience is too challenging to the existing construct, to the extent that the previous body of knowledge seems 'wrong', then a person will experience 'cognitive dissonance' and will respond in a number of ways that reveal real discomfort and various strategies of resistance (Hull, 1985, pp. 96–102).

Hull writes of the need to be right and the pain of learning: 'The need to be right carries with it the fear of being wrong. In the lives of many Christian adults these factors prevent learning. To be ready to learn is to be ready to admit that there is much one does not know, that one may not be entirely right. There is even the risk that one may be proved wrong' (p. 91). He comments that people vary a great deal in their ability to admit that they are wrong, and often the realization can result in a sense of being on the edge of something unstable, of being about to lose control. This can be a deeply worrying experience. For some people they simply cannot accept that they are wrong: to do so means that their whole personal construct would be damaged in unacceptable ways. Hull comments that such 'people prefer to be meaningfully wrong than nonsensically right' (p. 108), and often it is religious people, who have 'superordinate' constructs – 'ruling constructs of great generality and power around which commitment is focused' (p. 109) – that are most resistant to change. Often the feeling that will result will be a sense of guilt ('how could I think/do that? What sort of person must I be?') or a sense of threat. When feeling guilty or threatened, the new meaning or knowledge will often be isolated into its own subsystem and dissociated from the rest of the personal construct to prevent change from happening.

When new learning takes us to the limit of our understanding, and beyond – when something is incomprehensible, Hull says that the experience of being baffled is often the result, when it is difficult to incorporate the new with the existing structures of meaning. Bafflement indicates an impotence of knowledge, and can be very disturbing (p. 58), and comes when someone encounters a situation of shock or dissonance that is too much to bear. When the shock of the new is moderate, it is more likely that the cognitive dissonance will stimulate new discoveries and a healthy realignment of the whole system. To experience direct conflict between the new and existing self can stir real anger and pain, and in a learning situation the outcome for both the learner and the teacher can be disastrous.

When new learning cannot be incorporated, there will often be a withdrawal (p. 117) from the situation. Another technique Hull describes as 'thought-stopping', where 'an instant relief is provided from anxiety. The search has at last come to an end. Thought is renounced in joy.' Hull dismisses this strategy of avoiding the pain of learning: 'Wounds there are bound to be, as any thoughtful Christian consciousness today will recognize, but to escape from the pain by laying down the weapons of thought at the feet of the idol of comfort is no answer' (p. 121). Another response to challenging learning can be an ideological hardening (p. 125), where the construct will become ever less impervious to difference. Distractive strategies can be employed, and some examples are given below. Hull offers 'the obvious way out of these difficulties is an advance forward into the risk and pain of new learning', but he recognizes that 'the inhibitions, the doubts, the low morale and the fear of further cognitive shock make this a fearful prospect for many adults' (p. 133).

As I write this, I'm aware of thinking that it's other people who will be guilty of an inability to cope with the pain of learning. Of course it doesn't apply to me . . .

And so I am prompted to think of times when it has happened – when I have been unable to absorb new material because it has simply been too challenging.

Hull advocates a lightness of touch, and the importance of presenting new material with a certain humour. He argues for the necessity of allowing people room to play with new ideas, to entertain them without any threat of heavy commitment. For new things to be thought and tried out, particularly ideas that previously would have been unacceptable within the personal construct, safe exploration can be extremely helpful in lessening the anxiety, the threat and the guilt of religious adults. He says that autobiography, recalling in speech or writing, the ways in which a person's ideas and attitudes have developed, can be really helpful. His suggestions here emphasize how supervision can offer a playful space. The use of journal-writing, explored in the last chapter, can enable us to work with the anxiety of new experience and new learning.

Foskett and Lyall, in *Helping the Helpers*, stress the importance of recognizing that anxiety will be a prime state of mind in any learning situation (1990, p. 114). Their psychodynamic approach has real value, especially when it comes to reflecting upon the ways in which both supervisor and reflective practitioner can resist learning in an attempt to avoid the anxiety that can be an overwhelming element in training situations and lifelong learning. Within supervision both supervisor and reflective practitioner will engage at times in games of avoidance, games that enable each or both to side-step the uncomfortable processes of changing a deeply held attitude, or changing a way of doing things that seems natural and normal. For the sake of the relationship both might well end up colluding with each other to let both off the hook of gaining important, but difficult insights and development. Perhaps self-awareness is just too painful. There will be material for reflection that could be brought to supervision, but perhaps it is just not safe enough. And then, when that material is brought, it is too much for the supervisor to bear, too. So the suggestion is made that we go and have lunch instead, breaking the supervision contract.

Containing Anxiety

The establishment and maintenance of the working contract is an essential part of the supervisory relationship for this reason. It functions, more than anything, as the means of containment, the means whereby the anxiety of learning can be held and worked with, a way to allow the chaos of ministry to be contained. Both supervisor and reflective practitioner should be alert to the times and ways in which the contract is broken, or infringed, as this may well denote unconscious avoidance strategies at play that need attention for what they might reveal about the source of anxiety. It will be difficult to tackle such issues. Perhaps it might lead supervisor and reflective practitioner into areas of potential conflict.

Conflict

Conflict provokes anxiety in itself, and avoiding conflict can become a major reason why each or both play some game or another. But what is learnt in such a situation? Merely how to avoid conflict. Both reflective practitioner and supervisor will come away with an experience in which the learning is impaired, where to learn by reflection and reflexivity about dealing with conflict might be an extremely important lesson to learn.

Phillips and Pugh, writing about the process of academic supervision in their book *How to Get a PhD*, draw attention to the fact that men and women will often deal with conflict in different ways. They look to research which showed that women seem more concerned than men about the potential damage to interpersonal relationships that arguments might cause, with the result that men are much more likely to speak in seminars than women, and that women are more likely to expect to be criticized for expressing disagreement which inhibits them from expressing their true thoughts. The research showed that men who argue were regarded as rational, but women who argue are regarded as disagreeable, and unless it is within a relationship of equality, women will tend to avoid disagreement (Phillips and Pugh, 1993, p. 118). In a one-to-one situation, a male supervisor of a female reflective practitioner who has not worked with women before, might well feel inhibited about giving feedback in the belief that women are more emotional than men.

Have you been aware of a time when gender has made a difference to a learning situation? Describe what happened. How might it have been different?

The working contract becomes a crucial means of containing the anxiety and possible conflicts of learning, and any departure from the agreement needs careful consideration. If someone is late, or cancels – perhaps something important is being avoided. The value of adhering to a structure such as that described in Chapter 4 pays off for the indication it can give for unconscious deviation from the task of learning.

Games People Play

So how do supervisors and reflective practitioners avoid the anxieties and difficulties of learning new attitudes and skills and growing in self-awareness? Eric Berne in his book of popular psychology *Games People Play* defined a game as an 'ongoing series of complementary ulterior transactions, superficially plausible, but with a concealed motivation' (quoted in Foskett and Lyall, 1990, p. 119). We have already seen that the most likely 'concealed motivation' is the avoidance of anxiety and potential conflict provoked by the newness of a training situation, and by the challenge of gaining new competencies and having to change old habits. What, though, might the complementary ulterior transactions be? That they are complementary suggests that although the game may be initiated by one or other, the supervisor or reflective practitioner, the other will, at least to begin with, be taken in by the superficially plausible presenting behaviour, and respond, even collude with the game of avoidance. Kadushin, who first identified various games that people play in supervision, argued that to recognize a game for what it is enables the learning to move to a deeper, more significant level. He wrote:

> Perhaps another approach [apart from refusing to play or confrontation] is to share with the supervisee one's own awareness of what he is attempting to do but to focus neither on the dynamics of his behaviour nor on one's reaction to it but on the dynamics of his behaviour in playing games. These games have decided drawbacks for the supervisee in that they deny him the possibility of effectively fulfilling one of the essential principal purposes of supervision – helping him to grow professionally. The games frustrate the achievement of this outcome. In playing games the supervisee loses by winning. (quoted in Foskett and Lyall, 1990, p. 122)

So what games can be identified? The list that follows has been adapted from Hawkins and Shohet (2002, pp. 24–5) and Foskett and Lyall (1990, pp. 119ff.). Some games belong with the reflective practitioner, others with the supervisor. So what of the games the reflective practitioner might play?

In each of these games, think about how you, if you were supervisor, would respond.

- What do you think is the hidden agenda here?
- What would be a collusive response?
- What would be a challenging response?
- What would be a response that would take the learning further?

For example:
I've had the magazine article, a paper to write, family stuff to sort this week.

The hidden script here could be:
'I'm too busy to do the work you required me to do. And if you're unhappy about that, then you've got to appreciate that the other work/my family comes first.'

So how should the supervisor respond?

- 'That's all right. I understand. We'll rearrange the time. How long do you need?' (collusive)
- 'So do you use parish work as an excuse for getting out of doing the dishes at home?' (challenging)
- 'I think there's an issue here we need to explore about conflicting demands on your time.' (exploratory)

Given these different options that follow, think through what you consider to be the hidden script, and a collusive, challenging and exploratory response.

- You are the best supervisor I've ever had . . .
- Do you mind if, instead of talking about work this morning, I tell you about this personal problem I've got?
- It's so good to know that you're my friend. I know I can trust you not to say anything bad on my end of year report.
- If you knew postmodern critical theory like I know postmodern critical theory!
- What do you know about it anyway?
- I've got a little list.
- I did it like you told me!
- What you don't know won't hurt me.

Some of these games a reflective practitioner can play. There will be other ones. It is not only the reflective practitioner that can play games. The supervisor too may want to avoid the anxiety provoked by a new situation and new challenges, and might well present with his own games.

I wonder why you said that.
Hidden script: Help! This person is challenging me rather uncomfortably – is even disagreeing with me! Avoid the difficulty, quick, and give it a psychological spin at the same time. That always works.

How should the reflective practitioner respond?

- 'I said it because I want to know!'
- 'Well, I don't know really. I guess I shouldn't have. It seemed a good area to explore. But perhaps it wasn't.'
- 'Are you really saying you don't want to face that issue?'

One good question deserves another.
Hidden script: I haven't a clue how to respond to that problem/issue/question, but can't possibly admit my ignorance. So throw it back, quickly, and give yourself time to think!

How should the reflective practitioner respond?

- 'Are you asking me to do some work to answer the question myself because you don't know?'
- 'Ok, I'll see if I can find out by the next time we meet.'
- 'Will that give you time, too, to find out the answer?'

I can hardly catch my breath . . .
Hidden script: I'm so busy I haven't had time to think about our supervision session. Sorry! Can we postpone?

How should the reflective practitioner respond?

- 'Yes, that's fine. I've been busy too.'
- 'We could still meet. I've got some issues I want to explore. I don't mind if you just listen.'
- 'You get cross when I try to cancel our sessions. Why are you doing it to me?'

Games are played in order to sidestep some anxiety or issue that is not being confronted with honesty. They often reveal tensions that pull at the boundaries that hold the relationship, and threaten the contract that has been established so that anxiety can be contained and managed positively. Under pressure, the margins of the space will split and fragment if they are allowed to. It is the responsibility of the supervisor to sustain those boundaries and the contract that holds them secure.

We have identified the main sources of anxiety that are embedded in the processes and dynamics of learning. Tension and anxiety can also end up in the space of supervision because of the parallel process that was explored in Chapter 4 above. Here the presenting anxiety is not about new learning, but belongs somewhere else, within the practice of ministry itself. For example, a minister might come for supervision bearing some of the tension or nervousness of a funeral visit, or a fraught local residents' meeting and exhibit that tension unconsciously within the session. Distinguishing between the different, largely unconscious games and transferred feelings or behaviours falls to the supervisor, and again, often the best indicators of important material which requires further reflection is when the working agreement is threatened at its margins, or when the supervisor discerns transferred feelings that they can bring to light. When the boundaries that the contract has established are secure, that very security will allow difficult learning to emerge. If they are not secure, then learning will not proceed to any depth.

Defensive Personae

Foskett and Lyall identify certain personae that supervisors and reflective practitioners can adopt in order to defend themselves against the challenge of new learning (1990, pp. 127ff.).

The Preacher is someone who falls back on received truths and relies on other people's wisdom rather than taking the risk of being open to working it out for themselves. The Bible can be a useful tool for the preacher. Instead of a sensitive exploration of some issue, the answer is immediately gleaned and presented as a biblical text.

The Laissez-Faire Person is someone who, from lack of confidence or fear, uses extreme passivity as a defence. The supervisor will be content to let the reflective practitioner take the lead and will offer minimal guidance, often leading to intense frustration.

The Depend-On-Me Person will nurture an unhealthy over-dependence which inhibits the reflective practitioner from taking risks or exploring new challenges.

The Professor rationalizes and intellectualizes every situation and analyses with theories (methods of personality typing can be a popular choice of such theory, for example) any emotional content or personal stuff that threatens to challenge her.

So far we have looked at defensive strategies and personae that can be used to avoid the discomfort of new learning. Seeing such games and strategies for what they are, and being able to name them within supervision, can initiate deeper reflection that moves the mutual learning onto another level.

Do you see yourself in any of the above personae?

Collusion and Transference

Such roles often invite collusive responses. If the minister is someone who likes to be depended upon, then he will attract people who like to depend. If a reflective practitioner likes to preach, and tell people of the wisdom of others, then those sorts of people will be gathered in. The way the supervisor and reflective practitioner relate to one another can be a place where strong transferences happen. Hawkins and Shohet describe it thus:

The supervisory relationship is both more equal [than a counselling one] and more authoritative, as it contains a critical parent–child aspect. So supervisors are often not seen for who they are; sometimes they are given too much power, at other times they may be defensively seen as useless. Sibling rivalry can occur in terms of who can manage the client better, and this can come just as much from the supervisor as the supervisee. (2002, p. 25)

Parent–child transferences can occur, and so can other ones. The reflective practitioner may see the supervisor as the fount of all wisdom, and idealize her to the extent that the supervisor finds it impossible to be accepted as someone who fails or is vulnerable. Part of the eagerness to please that a student minister can feel can develop into stronger feelings and fantasies of a sexual nature, which can be extremely difficult to handle. Often such strong feelings can be a powerful defence against engagement with the learning processes. Sometimes they can be so powerful and seductive that the supervisor responds, flouting professional guidelines that put the responsibility with the dominant person in such situations.

We have considered anxiety as one of the key sources of resistance to learning. Another can be frustration, bordering on resentment at the way in which the learning contract is established and the lack of any real mutuality in the learning process. Much resistance to learning can be dissipated when the supervisor and the reflective practitioner take full responsibility for being proactive in what they want from the relationship. It helps if there is clarity about the key roles that the supervisor has – that of educator, manager and support – and the attendant authority that each component has is made explicit and is open for discussion at any point throughout the period of supervision. The more open each can be with the other in the supervisory relationship, the more can be gained from the encounter in terms of professional development. If the supervisor is able to model such a non-defensive openness, chances are the reflective practitioner will learn that way of being too, which will reap benefit in all areas and contexts of ministry.

Resistance for a Reason

So far we have looked at the different strategies that learners and supervisors can employ to resist learning. There is another sense in which resistance in learning can be apparent. There can be situations where a minister in training finds herself or himself struggling to hold onto a personal construct, a sense of identity in the face of a dominant culture, such as the church, which makes assumptions that dismiss or devalue that identity. This is not so much about new learning, though there may be ways in which new learning is blocked by the need to hold onto and defend a sense of threatened self. It may also be the case that the supervisor or organization needs to hear more clearly the perspective of others and learn from them. Many black people, gay people, people with disabilities, many women have brought and continue to bring their experience to the traditional structures and practices of the church to find themselves effectively silenced. Riet Bons-Storm (1996) has written of the way in which women can be categorized as 'incredible' – unbelievable – because their stories cannot find a place within the assumptions of counsellors and pastors who are unaware of their own dominant perspectives, and how they have construed their own framework as 'normal'. Such dominant people are deaf and blind to the experience of others whose stories do not fit within their frame. Bons-Storm, writing from a feminist perspective, argues how important, and difficult, it can be for women to sustain a sense of identity in the face of the disbelief and silencing they can encounter. Although she writes for women, her thinking can be extended to others.

It is important that the sort of resistance that a non-dominant person may offer in order to remain true to his identity is not confused with the games people play to avoid the anxiety of learning. Both can be seen as resistance. Indeed, sometimes a supervisor may well confuse the two. On one occasion a theological educator told me of a time when her colleagues on the staff of a theological college had become increasingly concerned about a black African student who was failing to hand in work as required. He seemed to be resisting the educational task. But after his wife delivered a child, it transpired that he was unable to tell anyone she was pregnant because that was not in accordance with the cultural conventions he and she were accustomed to. It had been a difficult pregnancy; she was lonely and he had been under a great deal of pressure he had not been able to share with the staff. What was interpreted as resistance by the college staff was a different sort of resistance, a cultural resistance to the dominant white milieu which didn't understand his background sufficiently. The staff and student were able, subsequently, to have an open discussion about the misunderstandings that had resulted, and an exploration of the learning that needed to happen both on the college staff's side, and the black ordinand's part, of how transcultural factors had led to confusions. Given the convention of privacy about pregnancy, how might the black student nevertheless have communicated to his tutor the pressure he was under at home? How would he deal with a similar situation when he was leading a congregation as its minister in the future?

Had you been this student's tutor, how would you have supervised subsequent exploration of the issues involved so that the student and the theological college learned from the situation? What questions would you ask in order to ensure that the issues were adequately addressed?

Different Sorts of Power

We have begun to explore the ways in which the space and dialogues of supervision are permeated with power in the sense that different perspectives and positions carry more or less dominant or subordinated voices, recalling how Bakhtin understood dialogue to be power-laden. Within a supervisory relationship, Hawkins and Shohet distinguish three different types of power that can be found (2002, p. 94).

- *Role power* is inherent in the role of supervisor. It will vary depending on the extent to which it is inscribed in the organizational setting of the supervision. If a student minister consults with a mentor whom they have chosen, the role power of that mentor will be less than that of a supervisor who has been selected by, for example, Anglican diocesan procedures, to have oversight of a three- or four-year training programme. As we have explored, an important aspect of role power is to oversee the establishment of the contract and boundaries of the space of supervision, so that there is enough safety that the anxiety of learning can be held, and risks of exploring failure and practising alternatives taken. Taking appropriate authority for this crucial aspect of role power is important. Kadushin says: 'the supervisor must accept, without defensiveness or apology the authority and related power inherent in his position. Use of authority may sometimes be unavoidable. The supervisor can increase its effectiveness if he feels, and can communicate, a conviction in his behaviour' (quoted in Hawkins and Shohet, 2002, p. 96).
- *Personal power* is the particular power that an individual has because of their expertise and experience. It is often consolidated by their personality. Many people remember an inspiring teacher, whose personal power was such that learning was an adventure and interesting compared to the dull teacher who had little or no personal power. Personal power can be augmented when the reflective practitioner wants to identify with the supervisor (p. 95).
- *Cultural power* is power that is derived from the dominant social and ethnic group. Hawkins and Shohet comment that 'In northern Europe a person with cultural power would be someone who was born within the white, western majority group. This power is emphasized if that person is male,

middle class, heterosexual and able-bodied' (pp. 94–5). This aspect of power is most important to grasp, especially if a supervisor is to enable the reflective practitioner to explore with self-reflexivity their own perspectives and positions within ministry as they engage in situations which are power-laden. The context of supervision can prove an extremely valuable place to enhance skills of working in transcultural situations, with the sense of 'culture' being the aspects of identity that are given and can be used as defining characteristics: gender, 'race' or ethnicity, sexuality, disability, class, for example. If someone is deaf, they might well describe themselves as belonging to a deaf culture. People of different gender will often claim that they see the world differently because of that gender. Most often those who do not consider themselves to be encultured in this way are exactly those who have cultural power as Hawkins and Shohet describe it above.

The ability to be self-reflexive and able to interrogate one's own positionality with regard to the appropriate use of authority and power, and then to model this to the reflective practitioner, can be extremely valuable. Attention to issues of power and dialogue needs to be there both in the material of ministry that is brought, and also in the relationship itself between supervisor and reflective practitioner, whether one-to-one or in a group. The space of supervision then becomes a place where all parties, with their differences, are enabled to participate in the learning. To do this effectively, issues of power and authority need to be on the table, and attention given to the ways in which dialogue is affected by differentials of power. Hawkins and Shohet remark:

The supervisory relationship is already complicated . . . because of the authority vested in the role of the supervisor. In working with difference, power dynamics are compounded because of the inequality of power between majority and minority groups . . . power invested in different roles, cultures and individual personalities comes together to make a complex situation which is nevertheless better explored than ignored or denied. (2002, p. 89)

There is no neutral position here: the reflective practitioner, and the supervisor, will perceive things differently depending on their cultural identity.

One way of analysing your cultural identity is to do a cultural genogram. Consider your own roots in terms of what you know about your family background and formative years.

How does your background continue to shape your present identity?

(A good resource for further exploration of such issues is Beckford, 2004.)

The purpose of this activity is to open up the growing awareness that each of us is embedded in culture, and the way we express that, with the different perspectives that contribute to our sense of self in the world, will have a crucial bearing on how we minister in a transcultural environment and understand why some resist the dominant perspectives of others. None of us is culturally neutral: we will always see the world from the particularities of our own standpoint, with our different assumptions and values. To grow in awareness of this means that we become increasingly sensitive in the ways we understand and negotiate cultural difference and resistance born of the reality of subordination. Hawkins and Shohet point out that 'to best facilitate this sensitivity we need not only to take an active interest in other cultures and areas of difference but also must never assume that we understand the client's cultural world. We can then start with an interest in finding out from the other while accepting our own not knowing' (2002, p. 103). A standpoint of curiosity and the ability not to know, not to make assumptions, but to be open in the face of different perspectives, enables learning between the supervisor and the reflective practitioner, setting the pattern for understanding diversity of perspective within the context of ministry.

To be reflexive within the supervisory relationship will affect the relationship itself. Instead of it being modelled as an apprenticeship, with the supervisor knowing all, and imparting knowledge 'top down', the relationship itself becomes a partnership, where responsibility for the learning is shared between each participant, as each learns together about the ways in which each holds and exercises authority and power. We are led back to the importance of setting a learning contract and initial conversations about ground rules in supervision, to create a milieu where the supervisor is more like a mentor than an expert. The expertise of the supervisor is apparent in how effectively she enables dialogue and exploratory, open conversation about resistance to learning, as a means of learning and growth in awareness, so that this becomes a constant element throughout ministry in a diverse world.

7

LEARNING TO COPE WITH THE DOWNSIDE

The last three chapters have focused on the space of supervision and how the material of ministry can be brought for reflection. We have explored the dialogues within living human documents and the ways in which new learning can be resisted, recognizing that change can provoke a powerful sense of anxiety and fear of failure.

In this chapter we return to three of our ministers who reflect upon the frustrations of ministry. Ministry can be dispiriting and keeping a sense of hope alive in the face of indifference and decline can prove overwhelming at times. To sustain lifelong learning throughout ministry is to face challenges and the risk of change, and to be prepared to cope with disappointment and failure that can demotivate and disable the very sense of vocation and engagement that lies at the heart of ministerial practice.

When I asked Geoff to write what disappointed him about his ministry, he described how decline made its impact upon church and the local community.

If there is one feature of church life with which I have to constantly contend it is the steady decline in the number of people attending worship and of a whole network of groups and activities which grew up around the church and its worship. Of course this decline is part of a general trend in the churches of Europe in the late twentieth and early twenty-first centuries, but it hits us here in particular ways. Our church was built and opened in 1960 on the back of a period of optimism and expansion for the churches in this country. A month before it was dedicated and opened for worship there were 475 communicants at the Easter services held in the dual purpose building which is now the church hall. That was the highest figure ever recorded and the trend has been consistently downhill since – we have barely reached 60 Easter communicants in any of the six years I have been at the church.

This decline in church life has paralleled what many people would see as a decline in the quality of the life of the local community. It certainly reflects the reality that the children of church members over the past 40 years have moved away from the estate, either because housing was not available locally or because of their own aspirations. The situation here can feel worse because (alone amongst our team ministry's churches) we have an early service of Holy Communion two hours before our main service. We feel, and appear, weaker than we actually are, and each group is easily swallowed up by the vast space of our church.

In addition, and like so many churches today, the age range of our congregation is a narrow one, with few people below 50 years of age. We have from the beginning failed to see the importance of attracting new people in sufficient numbers to sustain the church's life. Now that so many church members are in their seventies and eighties we have little chance of growing in significant numbers, or even replacing those who die or who are unable any more even to attend worship. A consequence of this is that there are fewer people to take on responsibility and they have more to do just to keep things going. They are tired of what they have to do and disheartened as well. So there have been moments in meetings of the church council in which it has felt as though no-one was willing for any initiative to be taken because of the demands it might place on them, and we have been enveloped by a blank and uneasy silence.

It has sometimes been hard not to feel that I am responsible for this situation or that is my failure, as it has seemed to me, to turn it round. It has often felt as though the decline has accelerated since I have been at the church. I have had to remind myself that whatever I might be able to do to help the church forward in this place, it is not up to me to get it right on my own.

Speaking with church members I have not tried to hide the difficulty of the task we face or the possibility that we might have to be ready to let go of the present pattern of church life and worship in order for the emergence of something new and more adapted to the world as it is it today (if only we knew what). In the face of people's disappointment and despair I have reminded them that we are still *here*, and that our worship and our pastoral care still go on and still speak of the love of God in Christ. I have offered my own confidence that the things we believe in and hold most dear are indeed of the greatest value to us and to the world around us. So it is important to do all that we do as well as we can in order that it may communicate the gospel.

I have sought to present as simply and as clearly as I can what I believe we are about, and to move forward only when enough people have felt ready to do so to sustain whatever we might be attempting to do at any particular time. Our church's situation is still fragile, but there are signs that we are becoming more focused and more hopeful, and that we are beginning to take things forward.

How do you respond to what Geoff writes?

How would you describe the health of your church?

Write something of your experience of facing bleak situations, where hope seemed fragile.

What resources or strategies do you use to keep going?

James writes from the experience of his curacy, but expresses some of the same sense of disappointment at how little difference his efforts seem to make.

I think I would describe myself as reasonably highly motivated, and unfortunately highly 'driven'. By this I mean that it is important for me to succeed, or at least get close to what I would perceive as the goal. This affects every element of my life and my ministry. But I would see no distinction between the two. I believe strongly that God has called me into church leadership and that is part of who I am, and whether I like it or not it affects every other part of my life . . .

For example, it happened while I was writing the diary and it happens a lot. We get homeless people and those struggling with addictions, particularly alcohol, knocking at the door at any time of the day or night. Initially we would feed and welcome them at any time, but it began to take its toll on married life, and now it has to be within certain hours, or they get turned away. Speaking honestly, it doesn't sit easily with me: there's a part of both Clare and me that would want to house, feed and welcome anyone, but we can't for our own sanity, we can't financially and actually it doesn't seem to benefit those concerned anyway. We try and get a balance of helping most people, but we invest to a greater extent with just a few people who we see more regularly. For me it is hard to get the balance right between saying 'this is family time' and 'this is work time': they overlap too easily. Sunday morning worship is both family time and work time – there is no easy distinction. Cell group is family time and work time, again no easy distinction . . .

When I read through my diary I realized that I really don't get the balance always right between work and family life. My day off, a Saturday, is too often taken up with last minute changes to a sermon, setting up the church, or dealing with someone at the door. This not only affects my personal well-being, but it affects my wife and daughter. It sounds simple, but the frequency with which I actually sit down and eat with my family is low, and it actually is both genuinely upsetting and worrying to acknowledge that. OK, we set Monday in stone to eat and pray together, but it isn't enough, and it is something I have every intention to sort out.

Sunday mornings, as I expressed in my diary, are hard work, and very stressful. I have become more accustomed to what's required of me, but I still find that Sunday is a drain, rather than a sustaining part of my life. I cannot see any way around it. I have shared out a large amount of the work I do, but during the service there are no musicians, few people able or willing to lead services and it's going to take time to train people.

But really this is where my greatest source of stress and worry is. I've been part of this church for over two years, and during that time our numbers have dropped slowly, but steadily through death, and people leaving the area. My whole experience of ministry is that of managing decline, not growth. The naïve, wet-behind-the-ears curate that I still am believed that I would be part of something that grew spiritually, numerically and in the level of engagement with the community that it was involved in. I am genuinely desperate to see the church thrive, and my deepest concern is to see those who are already members deepen their faith and relationship with Jesus, and see new people come to faith. I am not unrealistic, and didn't imagine that we would double our numbers in a week, but I did believe that through a combination of prayer, accessible worship and engagement with the community we would see growth, in its widest sense, and we haven't. And that hurts . . . a lot.

I suppose some of that is pride, wanting to be part of the leadership team that is involved in growth. Believing that by really working at my preaching, making it accessible, funny, interesting, challenging etc., it would make a difference. But I think that there is a large amount of pressure, particularly within the charismatic evangelical wing of the church that says that growth is the natural state of a living organism, and therefore a living church. That if your doing you job (prayer, preaching, visiting, community projects etc.) correctly then everything else will fit into place and growth will happen. My experience of ministry isn't that straightforward. Leading a church in a tough Urban Priority Area is actually very draining and growing a church is difficult. And whether I like to admit it or not, sometimes it is difficult not to sit back at the end of a long day and feel like you're failing.

If someone was to ask me about church life then I would never declare it as a failure – because it is neither healthy nor, in my more sane moments, do I think that it is a simple case of failure. The church has come a long way while I've been here. We've seen some amazingly special things happen, as well as some awful stuff. But at the end of the day I deal with this 'perceived area of failure' simply by trying desperately to cling to God's call to the ministry. And by trying not to listen very much to those who think they have the trite answers. Having described this part of my ministry as a failure, however, could give the wrong impression. I still have an amazingly strong sense of the privilege that it is to serve God in this way. Ninety per cent of the time I still get a real buzz out of talking and sharing with people in the life of this church.

The community project side of my job is probably the most fruitful in the sense that I have really been welcomed into meetings and listened to, as though I were an expert on the subject of community regeneration, which I am not, and I have tried to make that clear! But again it puts stress on my work life. Filling in forms feels like work avoidance. It isn't, and it takes a lot of time, but I actually would much rather be out visiting people in the community, particularly those who don't come to church. So frequently I will end up working stupidly long hours to do both, when really I can't sustain that amount of work for long without overdoing things.

I am constantly fighting a battle to get the balance right between church, community and personal life. If I have a day that is really quiet, where I have managed to visit all the people I needed to, there are no forms pending etc., then I so easily slip into feeling guilty for not working hard enough. But actually I need these quiet times to allow me the space to prepare for the more intense times.

If James came to you for supervision with the above extract from his journal, how would you be a critical friend to him?

What areas would you explore?

How would you help him towards new learning as he reflects here on his practice?

What biblical, theological or other resources would you use to reflect together on what James has written?

Roger writes about a different experience – not about the difficulty of living with ministry in a situation of decline. For him the sense of failure he writes about stems from a past event that obviously has 'stayed with him' as one that caused him regret.

I was once minister of a small church where the balance of power between two families was always a significant factor in the inner life of that church. There was so much that was very good about that church; it was beautifully kept, worship was meaningful, it welcomed visitors. Yet, under the surface there was an extremely delicate balance of power that had to be held with all the powers of diplomacy one could muster. At the worst times, just a look, or a word with one person but not another could actually be a factor that mushroomed into far greater significance and could be a balance of power issue affecting the life of the church. It was a sad canker rattling within the life of that church; it was known about in the community around the church and thus did inhibit its growth. The fairly simple task of asking someone to do a particular job, a very small thing in itself, had to be thought out against the big picture. I soon became conscious that the Church Council was not the place where the real power lay or where real decisions were made. People didn't really contribute much in those official meetings; they preferred to keep their heads below the parapet, lest there be repercussions later. For me the great disappointment was not that these people were 'bad' people, they weren't; they were good people caring and kind in their lives, effective for good in the places where they lived and worked. Yet somehow issues probably going back into the collective subconscious of a few generations back still had their power in the present. My two chief aims as their minister became to bring back power to the Church Council and to bring someone from neither of the two families into the leading role as Senior Church Steward.

I have many very happy memories of being minister of that church, and I think we succeeded somewhat in that first aim. Nevertheless, I think my overall disappointment and sense of failure was how the second aim was not, and perhaps could not be realized. A comparative newcomer agreed to serve as Senior Church Steward, a wise thoughtful person with a deep faith. What I hadn't realized was that she would become a 'whipping boy' for both sides and would bear greater hurt than perhaps she ever told me about. At one particularly tense time, she wanted to resign, but I persuaded her to continue which she agreed to do until the end of my ministry there. This she did, a real act of charity and faith, though I discovered that within a year of my moving on she had transferred to the other Methodist church in the town. I can understand this yet I still feel a sense of sadness that I exposed her to that hurt, and, I think, a sense of failure that I wasn't able to effect a greater and longer lasting reconciled life for that church. I suppose, however, there is that question as to how possible radical surgery is, during a five year ministry, in dealing with complicated conflicts that seem to have affected a few generations.

A sense of regret, such as Roger expresses, can remain with one for life. Often it can be accompanied by shame and a desire to keep failure hidden from colleagues and significant people within church structures for fear of exposure, of being seen to be incompetent.

If Roger had been coming to you whilst he was at the pastorate he describes above, how would you have helped him explore different ways of coping with the situation he faced? How could he have been enabled to explore different alternatives and different strategies?

How might he have been enabled to evaluate the effectiveness, or not, of different strategies he used?

If lifelong learning has as its goal the development of practical wisdom, or phronesis, then the ways in which disappointment and a sense of failure are dealt with is extremely important. Failures, disappointment and mistakes can be the most important source of new learning. To achieve this it becomes crucial that the space of supervision allows for the honest exploration of failure and disappointment so that alternative practice can be explored without fear of condemnation or judgement. The supervisor's ability to hold the space safely so that a sense of failure can be shared is paramount here. One of the most reassuring ways in which this can be attained is by the supervisor's own lack of defensiveness around their disappointment and failure; the ability to model honestly the times and occasions when she or he has acted in ways that were regretted.

Lifelong ministry, as the six living documents reveal, is to follow a path of life that commits one to a high degree of giving of oneself in public contexts. It can be to work with decline and disappointment, which it is not always easy to share with others. It can lead to exhaustion and a sense of 'burn-out' if care is not taken to find strategies of survival. It can be to endure a long Holy Saturday, not knowing if the promise of Easter is to become a reality. A Holy Saturday, when the hands of the living God are not perceived to be there; when it is a fearful thing to fall and not be caught.

Supervision can offer a strategy for survival. It can provide the space to rest, to reflect, to make sense of life and ministry, to begin to play again in the face of frustration and disappointment. It can be a place of safety and challenge, a place of lifelong learning.

CONCLUSION

To commit oneself to lifelong learning is to risk. It is to risk former certainties and habitual ways of doing things for the sake of discipleship. To be a disciple is to follow a path of life that calls for openness to change and a willingness to be transformed by the presence of a living God whose grace breaks through in the world. It is to see signs of the living God in the circumstances of life and ministry, to foster those signs so that others are empowered to flourish and build up the common life. I have drawn on the experiences of different ministers to enrich my reflection upon ministry in a changing world, where the impact of globalization challenges local churches to find new ways of meeting the needs of increasingly polarized communities.

The contexts of ministry in today's world are not straightforward: local faith communities become much more diverse, and patterns of care and welfare rely upon collaboration with different agencies and organizations. I have set the work of reflective practice and supervision within ministry that is offered in a complex world as experienced by ministers as they face challenges, joys and difficulties in their work.

I have explored the practice of supervision as a means to support lifelong learning and discipleship. I have understood it as space and time for reflection on life and ministry which becomes a regular discipline and is undertaken in a one-to-one relationship, or in a group, or by oneself – a place to practise the practice of ministry. We have looked at how techniques of writing a journal, and other texts can turn life into a 'living human document' which offers material for reflection. To enable reflection and learning, the space of supervision needs to have secure boundaries in order to let the challenge of learning, which can be discomforting at times, to be worked with and absorbed at deep rather than superficial levels.

The role of the supervisor, I have suggested, is to provide a facilitating environment which is both challenging and secure. To do this, a supervisor needs to be able to hold the space with some sense of oversight, and yet also be able to enter into a learning agreement that is agreed together and mutually respectful. Supervision is seen as the opportunity for both supervisor and reflective practitioner to learn. How the supervisor models the quality of listening, challenging and dialogue contributes to the implicit learning of the reflective practitioner, so that good, rather than bad, habits are gained. The supervisor needs, also, a particular practical wisdom and oversight to hold the space of supervision so that the anxieties of new learning are not avoided through various strategies and games of resistance.

I have seen supervision primarily as an educational method rather than a psychotherapeutic one, and as such I have shown how supervision can support recent trends in theological education that increasingly recognize the importance of reflective practice throughout ministry. I have considered the goal of theological education and supervision in terms of identity, and especially ministerial identity. Instead of using the language of 'formation', which strikes me as static and complete, 'once formed, forever formed', I have thought about identity as something that is always changing in dialogue with others, in life and in different situations. I have developed the view that one's identity is always moving onwards, following a path of life, engaged with others, always in community, in dialogue with and from different standpoints and perspectives. To be in lifelong dialogue with others or with oneself as another is also to recognize that dialogue, and therefore one's identity, is always embedded in relationships that are power-laden.

The goal of lifelong learning is not, I have argued, a sense of arrival, of 'formation', but the pursuit of phronesis or practical wisdom, *knowing in action by reflection upon practice.* I have stressed that lifelong learning is a journey and a path of life. It is to be open and willing to learn in the encounter with different people and in different circumstances, and to have the desire to reflect upon the practice of life and ministry. Supervision can provide the space and time to fall into the hands of the living God and face, in safety, the challenge of change and our all-too-human fear of the new, for the sake of a better world.

BIBLIOGRAPHY

Alibhai-Brown, Yasmin (2001), *Mixed Feelings: The Complex Lives of Mixed-Race Britons*, London, The Women's Press.

Atherton, John (2003), *Marginalization*, London, SCM Press.

Bakhtin, Mikhail M. (1996), *The Dialogic Imagination: Four Essays*, ed. Michael Holquist, trans. Caryl Emerson and Michael Holquist, Austin, University of Texas Press.

Ballard, Paul and Pritchard, John (1996), *Practical Theology in Action: Christian Thinking in the Service of Church and Society*, London, SPCK.

Beckford, Robert (2004), *God and the Gangs: An Urban Toolkit for Those Who Won't be Sold Out, Bought Out or Scared Out*, London, Darton, Longman & Todd.

Bernauer, James, and Carrette, Jeremy, eds (2004), *Michel Foucault and Theology: The Politics of Religious Experience*, Aldershot and Burlington, Ashgate.

Bolton, Gillie (2003), *Reflective Practice: Writing and Professional Development*, London, Thousand Oaks and New Delhi, Paul Chapman.

Bons-Storm, Riet (1996), *The Incredible Woman: Listening to Women's Silences in Pastoral Care and Counseling*, Nashville, Abingdon Press.

Brierley, Peter (2000), *The Tide is Running Out: What the English Church Attendance Survey Reveals*, London, Christian Research Association.

Bunting, Madeleine (2004), *Willing Slaves: How the Overwork Culture is Ruling our Lives*, London, HarperCollins.

Burgess, Neil (1998), *Into Deep Water: The Experience of Curates in the Church of England*, Bury St Edmunds, Kevin Mayhew Ltd.

Burr, Vivien, and Butt, Trevor (2000), *Invitation to Personal Construct Psychology*, London, Whurr.

Cameron, Helen, Richter, Philip, Davies, Douglas and Ward, Frances (2005), eds, *Studying Local Churches: A Handbook*, London, SCM Press.

Castells, Manuel [1997], (2004), *The Power of Identity*, vol. 2 of *The Information Age: Economy, Society and Culture*, Oxford, Blackwell.

Castells, Manuel [1998], (2000), *End of Millennium*, vol. 3 of *The Information Age: Economy, Society and Culture*, Oxford, Blackwell.

Coffey, Amanda (1999), *The Ethnographic Self: Fieldwork and the Representation of Identity*, London, Sage.

Dalton, P. and Dunnet, G. (2000), *A Psychology for Living*, Farnborough, EPCA Publications.

Diocese of Coventry (2002), *From Ordination to Second Post*, Coventry, UK: Diocese of Coventry.

Ekstein, R., and Wallerstein, R. S. (1972), *The Teaching and Learning of Psychotherapy*, New York, International Universities Press.

Flyvbjerg, Bent (2001), *Making Social Science Matter: Why Social Inquiry Fails and How It Can Succeed Again*, Cambridge, Cambridge University Press.

Foskett, John, and Lyall, David [1988], (1990), *Helping the Helpers: Supervision and Pastoral Care*, London, SPCK.

Foucault, Michel [1975], (1991), *Discipline and Punish: The Birth of the Prison*, trans. by A. Sheridan, London, Penguin.

Fransella, F., ed. (2003), *The International Handbook of Personal Construct Psychology*, Chichester, John Wiley.

Fransella, F. and Dalton, P. [1990], (2000), *Personal Construct Counselling in Action*, 2nd edn, London, Sage.

Freire, Paulo (1970), *Pedagogy of the Oppressed*, Harmondsworth, Penguin.

Fryer, Peter (1984), *Staying Power: The History of Black People in Britain*, London and Boulder, Pluto Press.

Gerkin, Charles V. (1984), *The Living Human Document: Re-Visioning Pastoral Counseling in a Hermeneutical Mode*, Nashville, Abingdon Press.

Giddens, Anthony [1991], (2003), *Modernity and Self-Identity: Self and Society in the Late Modern Age*, Cambridge, Polity Press in association with Blackwell.

Graham, Elaine (1996), *Transforming Practice: Pastoral Theology in an Age of Uncertainty*, London and New York.

Green, Laurie [1990], (2000), *Let's Do Theology*, London, Mowbray.

Hawkins, Peter, and Shohet, Robin, *Supervision in the Helping Professions*, Buckingham, Open University Press.

Hull, John M. (1985), *What Prevents Christian Adults from Learning?*, London, SCM Press.

Ind, Jo (2003), *Memories of Bliss: God, Sex, and Us*, London, SCM Press.

Kadushin, A., *Supervision in Social Work*, New York, Columbia University Press.

Kelly, George (1955), *The Psychology of Personal Construct Theory*, New York, Norton.

Kolb, D. (1984), *Experiential Learning as the Science of Learning and Development*, Englewood Cliffs, Prentice-Hall.

Kristeva, Julia (1991), *Strangers to Ourselves*, trans. Leon Roudiez, New York, Columbia University Press.

Lash, Nicholas (2004), *Holiness, Speech and Silence: Reflections on the Question of God*, Aldershot and Burlington, Ashgate.

Lynch, Gordon (2002), *After Religion: Generation X and the Search for Meaning*, London, Darton, Longman & Todd.

Miller-McLemore, Bonnie J. (1996), 'The Living Human Web: Pastoral Theology at the Turn of the Century' in *Through the Eyes of Women: Insights for Pastoral Care*, ed. Jeanne Stevenson Moessner, Minneapolis, Augsburg Fortress Press.

Mission Shaped Church: Church Planting and Fresh Expressions of Church in a Changing Context (2004), London, Church House Publishing.

Moon, Jennifer A. (2004), *A Handbook of Reflective and Experiential Learning: Theory and Practice*, London and New York, Routledge-Falmer.

Osborn, Lawrence (1988), *Dear Diary: An Introduction to Spiritual Journalling*, Nottingham, Grove Books.

Pearce, Lynne (1994), *Reading Dialogics*, London, Edward Arnold.

Phillips, Estelle M. and Pugh, D. S. (1993), *How to Get a PhD: A Handbook for Students and their Supervisors*, Buckingham, Open University Press.

Polanyi, M., *Knowing and Being* (1969), ed. M. Grene, Chicago: University of Chicago Press.

Ricoeur, Paul, *Oneself as Another* (1994), trans. Kathleen Blamey, Chicago and London, University of Chicago Press.

Sandercock, Leonie (text) and Lyssiotis, Peter (images) (2003), *Cosmopolis II: Mongrel Cities in the 21st Century*, London and New York, Continuum.

Schön, Donald (1983), *The Reflective Practitioner*, San Francisco, Jossey-Bass.

Schön, Donald (1987), *Educating the Reflective Practitioner: Toward a New Design for Teaching and Learning in the Professions*, San Francisco, Jossey-Bass.

Schreiter, Robert (2002), *The New Catholicity: Theology Between the Global and the Local*, New York, Orbis.

Smith, Anna (1996), *Julia Kristeva: Readings of Exile and Estrangement*, London, Macmillan Press.

Stam, Robert (1989), *Subversive Pleasures: Bakhtin, Cultural Criticism, and Film*, Baltimore and London, Johns Hopkins University Press.

Stokes, Allison (1985), *Ministry After Freud*, New York, Pilgrim Press.

Storrar, Will (2005), 'Found in Space: The Local Church as Place', in *Studying Local Churches: A Handbook*, edited by Helen Cameron and others, London, SCM Press.

Taylor, John V. (1972), *The Go-Between God: The Holy Spirit and the Christian Mission*, London, SCM Press.

Volf, Miroslav (1996), *Exclusion and Embrace: A Theological Exploration of Identity, Otherness, and Reconciliation*, Nashville, Abingdon Press.

Walton, Heather and Hass, Andrew W., eds. (2000), *Self/Same/Other: Re-visioning the Subject in Literature and Theology*, Sheffield, Sheffield Academic Press.

Ward, Graham [1996], (2000), *Theology and Contemporary Critical Theory*, London, Macmillan Press.

Winnicott, Donald W. [1971], (1999), *Playing and Reality*, New York and London, Routledge.

Young, Iris Marion (2000), *Inclusion and Democracy*, Oxford, Oxford University Press.

Further Reading

Austin, Michael J. and Hopkins, Karen, eds (2004), *Supervision as Collaboration in the Human Services: Building a Learning Culture*, London.

Barnes, Gill G., Down, Gwynneth and McCann, Damian (2000), *Systemic Supervision: A Portable Guide for Supervision Training*, London: Jessica Kingsley Publishers.

Carroll, Michael and Tholstrup, Margaret, *Integrative Approaches to Supervision*, London, Jessica Kingsley Publishers, 2001.

Jacobs, Michael, ed. (1996), *In Search of Supervision*, Buckingham, Open University Press.

Lahad, Mooli (1999), *Creative Supervision: The Use of Expressive Arts Methods in Supervision and Self-Supervision*, London and Philadelphia, Jessica Kingsley Publishers.

Pritchard, Jackie, ed. (1995), *Good Practice in Supervision: Statutory and Voluntary Organisations*, London and Philadelphia, Jessica Kingsley Publishers.

Shipton, Geraldine, ed. (1997), *Supervision of Psychotherapy and Counselling: Making a Place to Think*, Buckingham and Philadelphia, Open University Press.

INDEX OF NAMES AND SUBJECTS

ACCM 22 72ff, 79, 80
ACPE 14
Administration 22, 31, 38
Alterity 17, 98, 101, 103
Ambiguity 87, 100
Anxiety 7, 33, 70, 115, 125,
 153, 154, 157ff, 167, 169, 173
Appraisal 16, 93, 130
Aristotle 2, 16, 131
Assessment 16, 74 n6, 77, 93,
 109ff, 148
Asylum seekers 41, 44, 57
Atherton, J. 17, 54, 56
Attitudes 86, 130, 132, 158, 160
Autobiography 129, 158
Avoidance 158, 159, 160, 161,
 178 see Anxiety, resistance

Bakhtin, M. M. 7, 133ff, 168
Baptist Union 71
Beginning Public Ministry 74 n6,
 76, 77
Bereavement xi, 36, 57, 84
Boisen, A. 13ff, 130, 152
Bolton, G. 13, 69, 92, 130ff,
 145, 147ff
Bons-Storm, R. 167
Boundaries 88ff, 93, 100, 103,
 105, 106ff, 111, 129, 163ff,
 169, 183
Bunting, M. 12
Burgess, N. xii, 106

Cabot, R. 13ff
Cameron, H. vii, 34 n1, 58
Capitalism 51ff, 58, 62,
 see Globalization

Castells, M. 52ff, 56, 58, 60ff
Christian scripture 74, 80
Christian tradition 15, 80
Church Army 9, 46ff
Church buildings 21, 30, 34, 36,
 40ff, 58ff, 174
Church of England xii, 6, 27,
 65, 71ff, 77, 79, 81ff
Church of Scotland 9, 35, 71
Class 55, 132, 142, 170
Clinical pastoral education xiii,
 13ff, 119, 128, 129
Clinical rhombus 7, 112f, 117,
 120, 128
Coffey, A. 140ff
Cognitive dissonance 156ff
Collaborative ministry 16, 57,
 77, 78, 79, 80, 135,182
Collusion 161, 162, 165
Communication xi, 7, 17, 21,
 51ff, 57, 64, 79, 89, 97, 98,
 130ff, 138, 140, 142ff,
 see Information Age
Communities of faith 11,17, 58,
 61,182
Community work 22, 24
Competencies xi, 80, 111, 160
Confidentiality 107ff
Conflict 27, 49, 63, 70, 75, 99,
 157, 159ff, 180
Consultation xiii, 23, 77, 114
Continuing ministerial
 education 13, 74 n6, 82, 86,
 124
Contract 6, 105ff, 158, 159ff,
 164, 166, 169, 172

Counselling xi, 15, 16, 60, 106ff, 112, 116, 165
Counter-transference 112
Creative writing 13, 129, 147
Crime 41, 45, 56, 57
Critical friend 144, 149, 179
Cultural genogram 171
Culture 1, 17, 53, 62, 63, 75, 88, 90, 98, 122, 134, 136ff, 140, 142, 167, 170, 171
Curacy xi, xii, xiii, 77, 82, 85, 175

Decline 8, 11, 43, 54, 173ff, 177, 179, 181
Defensive personae 164ff
Defensiveness 3, 93, 169, 181
Democracy 54
Deprivation 20, 34, 54, 60
Desire 4, 7, 77, 100, 139, 143, 144, 180, 184
Dialogical theory 7, 133
Dialogue 7, 16ff, 56, 87, 88, 94, 95, 98, 100ff, 129ff, 133, 135, 136ff, 143ff, 148, 149, 152, 153, 168ff, 183
Difference 6, 7, 18, 19, 63, 78, 89, 90, 94, 95, 98ff, 129, 131, 132, 136ff, 170ff
Differentiated solidarity 55
Disability 79, 132, 170
Disappointment 8, 11, 98, 110, 173ff
Discrimination 12, 79
Distance learning 19
Diversity 62, 63, 72, 75, 80, 94, 95, 134, 135, 172
Dominance 18, 51, 56, 137, see Power, subordination
Dress 140ff
Drugs 45, 56

Ecumenism 22, 24, 61, 79
Education xii, xiii, 1ff, 6, 8, 13ff, 19, 53, 65ff, 93, 111, 132, 150, 154, 168, 183
Email 17, 23, 25, 33, 47, 48, 49, 64, 124, 130, 147

Emotion 7, 68, 85, 115, 141, 150ff, 153, 160, 165
Empowerment 1, 56, 80, 182
Engagement 7, 10, 27, 52, 54, 57ff, 72, 73, 75, 79, 81, 82ff, 89, 103, 106, 143, 166, 177
Ethnography 140, 148
Exclusion 53ff, 57, 99ff
Exposure 154, 180

Facilitating environment 6, 88ff, 93, 103, 105, 129, 153, 183
Facilitator 77, 117, 124, 125
Failure 3, 8, 94, 110, 147,153, 154, 169, 173ff
Fear 3, 7, 11, 12, 61, 63, 108, 109, 110, 136, 150, 153ff, 156, 157, 165, 173ff, 180, 181, 184
Flyvbjerg, B. 3, 16, 69, 131
Formation 16, 17, 71 n3, 72, 74, 74 n 6, 79, 80, 81, 87, 100, 102, 134, 135, 139, 141, 183, 184
Formation for Ministry within a Learning Church/the Hind Report 74, 80, 81
Foskett, J. vii, xiii, 5, 67, 88, 112, 115, 158, 160, 161, 164
Foucault, M. 18
Freire, P. 6, 65, 66, 73, 75
Fresh expression of church 9, 46, 50
Fundamentalism 12

Games people play 160ff, 167
Gender 55, 79, 142, 160, 170
Generation X 12
Generosity 94, 98, 101
Gerkin, C. V. 14, 15
Giddens, A. 131
Globalization 5, 56, 60, 182
'Good-enough' 88, 91, 93, 103, 153
Graham, E. vii, 3, 17, 61, 62, 64

Heteroglossia 133ff
Hind Report 74, 80, 81

Holy Spirit 72, 80, 94ff, 139
Homelessness 41, 176
Housing estates 20, 21
Hull, J. 1ff, 153ff

Identity 4, 16ff, 56, 61, 63, 64,
    76, 94, 99ff, 130ff, 147, 151,
    152, 153, 167, 170, 171, 183
Inclusivity 12, 54, 55, 56, 60,
    63, 95
Ind, J. 150, 151
Information age 52
Internal dialogue 7, 18, 135
Internet 1, 32, 53, 64, 123
Intimacy 143ff
Islam 12

Journal 7, 9, 13, 19, 20, 62, 68,
    70, 85, 129, 130, 132, 144ff,
    154, 158, 179, 182
Judaism 12

Kadushin, A. 161, 169
Kelly, G. 19, 155
Kenosis 99, 101
Knowledge xi, 1, 6, 12, 65ff, 82,
    86, 128, 131ff, 152, 155ff, 172
Kolb, D.A. 6, 67ff
Kristeva, J. 94, 101ff

Leadership 11, 28, 58, 79, 80,
    176, 177
Levinas, E. 94, 98ff, 138ff
Listening 6, 56, 94, 96, 105,
    118, 129, 135, 146, 183
Living human documents xiii,
    7ff, 13ff, 18, 19, 20ff, 56, 60,
    128, 129ff, 145ff, 173
Living human webs 11
Local authorities 23, 45, 55, 114
Locality 33, 57, 58, 61
Lyall, D. vii, 5, 67, 88, 112, 115,
    158,160,161, 164

Marginalization 54
Mentoring 71, 88, 144
Methodism 9, 22, 28, 33, 41,
    71, 180

Mission and Ministry 74, 79
Moon, J. 13, 66, 68, 69, 93, 109,
    130, 146ff, 155

Network society 17, 47, 52, 53,
    55, 56, 57, 64, 114, 173
New Age spirituality 12
Non-dominance 142, 167

Oversight 16, 77, 82, 87, 93,
    103, 169, 183

Parallel process 7, 115, 116, 164
Pastoral 11, 13, 14, 15, 23, 24,
    25, 48, 77, 78, 83, 84, 107,
    113, 175
Performative ministry 17, 59,
    62, 64
Personal construct theory 19, 155
Phronesis 3, 16, 131, 136, 181,
    184
Placement learning xii
Play 6, 7, 87ff, 102ff, 110, 147,
    150, 158, 160ff, 181
Polanyi, M. 6, 65
Polarization 52, 53, 57
Portfolio 10, 13, 19, 82, 85, 86,
    93, 130
Poverty 52, 53, 55, 57
Power 7, 11, 18, 53, 54, 56, 58,
    60, 64, 66, 92, 97, 99, 104,
    113, 116, 119, 121, 127, 132,
    133, 136ff, 142, 153, 156,
    166, 168ff, 179ff, 183,
    see Dominance, subordination
Practical theology xii, 67
Practice xi, xiii, 2, 3, 6ff, 59ff,
    67ff, 75, 81ff, 86, 87, 90ff,
    98ff, 105, 107, 111ff, 119,
    121, 127, 128, 129ff, 137,
    143, 146ff, 152, 154, 164,
    167, 173, 179, 181ff
Prayer 16, 25, 26, 30, 32, 36, 39,
    44, 47, 60, 106, 126, 127, 135,
    136, 144, 149, 177
Psychotherapy 91
Public 25, 46, 58, 63, 142, 143,
    154, 181

'Race' 55, 79, 170
Reflection xiff, 2ff, 7, 13, 15, 16,
  18ff, 67ff, 74, 80ff, 86, 92ff,
  97, 99, 102, 108, 111, 113,
  128, 129ff, 143ff, 148ff, 154ff,
  158, 159, 164, 165, 173, 182ff
  see Theological reflection,
  Reflective practice, Reflexivity
Reflective practice xiii, 8, 14, 64,
  71, 75, 81, 87, 92, 137, 147,
  148, 152, 182, 183
Reflective writing 13
Reflexivity 92, 131, 137, 142,
  143, 144, 159, 170
Regional training centres 80
Resistance 7, 8, 56ff, 116, 153ff,
  166, 167ff, 183
Role play 14, 117, 118, 121
Rural ministry 24ff

Sanctus1 9, 10, 46ff
Sandercock, L. 58, 61, 63, 64
Schön, D. 6, 69, 70
Schreiter, R. 51ff, 56ff, 60ff
Self-awareness 77, 107, 128,
  142, 158, 160
Sexuality 102, 132, 142, 143,
  166, 170
Skills xi, xiii, 1, 2, 15, 18, 38,
  70, 71, 74, 77, 80, 83, 86, 93,
  94, 103, 142, 143, 152, 160,
  170
Social analysis xii, 52, 74
Socialism 51, 52
Spiritual direction 15, 88, 144
Splitting 114
Storrar, W. 34 n 1, 58, 59
Subordination 137, 168, 171
Supervision xiii, 2, 5ff, 15ff, 36,
  51, 65, 71, 75, 77, 78, 82, 85,
  87, 88ff, 93ff, 97, 99, 102ff,
  105ff, 129ff, 144, 149, 153,
  154, 158, 159, 161, 163ff,
  168, 169, 170, 172, 173, 179,
  181, 182ff
Supervisor xii, xiii, 2, 7, 13, 14,
  16, 67, 71, 76, 77, 79, 81, 82,

87, 88, 93ff, 99, 102ff, 105ff,
  129, 155, 158ff, 181, 183

Taylor, J.V. 6, 94ff, 129, 136,
  140
Team ministry 20, 23, 145, 174
Theological education xiii, 1, 2,
  6, 8, 11, 14, 19, 65ff, 111, 183
Theological reflection xiii, 15,
  67, 99, 102, 121, 128, 146, 151
Therapy 16, 91, 112
Training xi, xii, 2, 14, 16, 17,
  41, 42, 71, 76ff, 87, 110ff,
  124, 155, 158, 160, 167, 169
Transculturalism 132, 168, 170,
  171
Transference 112, 165, 166
Trinity 18, 75, 76, 94, 97, 101,
  102

UKACPE 14
Uncertainty 75, 87, 92, 114, 186
United Reformed Church xii,
  22, 71
Urban ministry 46, 51, 52, 54,
  58, 63, 177, 185

Verbatim report xiii, 7, 10, 13,
  14, 110, 117ff, 125, 128,
  129ff, 147
Video recording 43, 44, 129
Violence 25, 52, 62, 100
Visiting 25, 31, 40, 59, 106,
  177, 178
Volf, M. 94, 99ff, 129
Voluntary organizations 12, 116
Vulnerability 94, 98, 142

Walton, Heather vii, 139
Winnicott, D.W. 6, 88ff, 103,
  129
Worship xi, 22, 24, 25, 31, 32,
  34, 35, 36, 39, 42, 50, 52, 56,
  58, 60, 64, 83, 173, 174, 175,
  176, 177, 179

Young, Iris Marion 54, 55